GANDHI ON NON-VIOLENCE

D0121948

By Thomas Merton

THE ASIAN JOURNAL OF THOMAS MERTON
GANDHI ON NON-VIOLENCE
THE GEOGRAPHY OF LOGRAIRE
NEW SEEDS OF CONTEMPLATION
RAIDS ON THE UNSPEAKABLE
SELECTED POEMS
THE STRANGE ISLANDS
THE WAY OF CHUANG TZU
THE WISDOM OF THE DESERT
ZEN AND THE BIRDS OF APPETITE

Published by
New Directions

GANDHI
ON NON-VIOLENCE

SELECTED TEXTS
FROM MOHANDAS K. GANDHI'S
Non-Violence in Peace and War

EDITED,
WITH AN INTRODUCTION, BY
THOMAS MERTON

A NEW DIRECTIONS PAPERBOOK

First published as New Directions Paperbook No. 197 in 1965

This book is published by the permission of the Navajivan Trust, P. O. Navajivan, Ahmedabad-14 (India), which controls the copyright in all works by M. K. Gandhi.

Library of Congress catalog card number: 65-15672
(ISBN: 0-8112-0097-3)
Manufactured in the United States of America.

New Directions books are published for James Laughlin
by New Directions Publishing Corporation,
333 Sixth Avenue, New York 10014

SEVENTH PRINTING

CONTENTS

C   24

Everyone who hates his brother is a murderer.

I JOHN, 3:15

Men who fear to make the sacrifice of love will have to fight.

TOYOHIKO KAGAWA

The great tasks of magnanimous men:—to establish with truth, justice, charity and liberty, new methods of relationships in human society—the task of bringing about true peace in the order established by God. We publicly praise such men and earnestly invite them to persevere in their work with ever greater zeal. It is an imperative of duty; it is a requirement of love.

POPE JOHN XXIII, *Pacem in Terris*

AN INTRODUCTION TO

SELECTIONS FROM GANDHI

Gandhi and the One-Eyed Giant

The white man, says Laurens Van Der Post(1) came into Africa (and Asia and America for that matter) like a one-eyed giant, bringing with him the characteristic split and blindness which were at once his strength, his torment, and his ruin. With his self-isolated and self-scrutinizing individual mind, Western man was master of concepts and abstractions. He was the king of quantity and the driver of those forces over which quantitative knowledge gave him supremacy without understanding. Because he ruled matter without understanding it, he faced his bodily self as an object which he could not comprehend though he could analyze and tamper with its every part. He submitted to passions which, though he no longer regarded them as devils, were nevertheless inscrutable and objective forces flying at him from the dark outside the little circle illumined by a pragmatic and self-complacent moral reason. The one-eyed giant had science without wisdom, and he broke in upon ancient civilizations which (like the medieval West) had wisdom without science: wisdom which transcends and unites, wisdom which dwells in body and soul together and which, more by means of myth, of rite, of contemplation, than by scientific experiment, opens the door to a life in which the individual is not lost in the cosmos and in society but found in them. Wisdom which made all life sacred and meaningful—even that which later ages came to call secular and profane.

It is true that neither the ancient wisdoms nor the modern sciences are complete in themselves. They do not stand alone. They call for one another. Wisdom without science is unable to penetrate the full sapiential meaning of the created and material cosmos. Science without wisdom leaves man enslaved to a world of unrelated objects in which there is no way of discovering (or creating) order and deep significance in man's own pointless existence. The vocation of modern man was to bring about their union in preparation for a new age. The marriage was wrecked on the rocks of the white man's dualism and of the inertia, the incomprehension, of ancient and primitive societies. We enter the post-modern (perhaps the post-historic!) era in total disunity and confusion. But while the white man has always, naturally, blamed the traditional ancient cultures and the primitive "savage" whom he never understood, it is certainly clear that if the union of science and wisdom has so far not been successful it is not because the East would not listen to the West: the East has been all too willing to listen. The West has not been able to listen to the East, to Africa, and to the now practically extinct voice of primitive America. As a result of this the ancient wisdoms have themselves fallen into disrepute and Asia no longer dares listen to herself!

The split of the European mind has become universal. All men (says L. L. Whyte) are caught in the "fundamental division between deliberate activity organized by static concepts, and the instinctive and spontaneous life." (2) This dissociation, which was fruitful in the Renaissance, has now reached a point of mad development, of "behavior patterns unrelated to organic needs" and a "relentless passion for quantity" . . . "uncontrolled industrialism and excess of analytical thought" . . . "without the catharsis of rhythmic relaxation or satisfying achievement." (3)

> This [Whyte continues] is the moment of uninhibited perversions which can now ally themselves with technical power . . . in a brief period of dominance. This short reign of Antichrist depends on the fusion of two principles which are both vicious because they represent only a part of European or Western human nature: instinctive vitality distorted into sadism, and differentiating human vitality distorted into quantitative expansion. (4)

Whyte was writing this in the days of Hitler, Mussolini, and Stalin, at the beginning of the Second World War. The "short" reign of Antichrist would soon, he believed, give way to a reign of light, peace, harmony, and reconstruction. The end of the war would begin a better era. Or at least so he hoped, though not without reservations, for he added: "one more dark decade would disprove my judgment, revealing a rot deeper than I have seen." (5) We are now in the third dark decade since his words were written.

Ananda Coomaraswamy, writing about the same time as L. L. Whyte, viewed the sickness of civilization in more religious terms, and with much the same seriousness. The problem of the whole world was the problem of Western man: for everywhere the one spiritual illness was now rampant, and malignancies, which in the West were perhaps endemic, were proliferating in the most alarming fashion in the East and in Africa.

"East and West," Coomaraswamy wrote, "are at cross purposes only because the West is determined, i.e., at once resolved and economically 'determined,' to keep on going it knows not where, and it calls the rudderless voyage 'Progress.' " (6)

He wrote before the days of Red China and of postwar Japan, both of which now lead scores of other nations in carrying the logic of the Western split to its most extreme dissociation. Today it is not only the

2

West that is "determined" on its rudderless voyage; all, down to the newest African nation, are in the same centrifugal flight, and the itinerary points to outer space.

The question remains the same. It is a crisis of *sanity* first of all. The problems of the nations are the problems of mentally deranged people, but magnified a thousand times because they have the full, straight-faced approbation of a schizoid society, schizoid national structures, schizoid military and business complexes, and, need one add, schizoid religious sects. "We are at war with ourselves," said Coomaraswamy, "and therefore at war with one another. Western man is unbalanced, and the question, Can he recover himself? is a very real one." (7)

The question is all the more urgent now that it concerns not only Western man but everybody.

There have of course been spurious attempts to bring East and West together. One need not review all the infatuated theosophies of the nineteenth century. Nor need one bother to criticize the laughable syncretisms which have occupied the talents of publicists (more often Eastern than Western) in which Jesus, Buddha, Confucius, Tolstoy, Marx, Nietzsche, and anyone else you like join in the cosmic dance which turns out to be not Shiva's but just anybody's. However, the comparison of Eastern and Western religious philosophy is, in our time, reaching a certain level of seriousness and this is one small and hopeful sign. The materials for a synthesis of science and wisdom are not lacking.

One of the most significant facts about the life and vocation of Gandhi was his discovery of the East through the West. Like so many others of India, Gandhi received a completely Western education as a young man. He had to a great extent renounced the beliefs, the traditions, the habits of thought, of India. He spoke, thought, and acted like an Englishman, except of course that an Englishman was precisely what he could never, by any miracle, become. He was an alienated Asian whose sole function in life was to be perfectly English without being English at all: to prove the superiority of the West by betraying his own heritage and his own self, thinking as a white man without ceasing to be "a Nigger." The beauty of this (at least to Western minds) was that it showed Western culture to be a pearl of such great price that one could reasonably sell the whole of Asia in order to acquire it, even though the acquisition was not that of a new being, or even of a new identity, but only of a new suit.

Gandhi was unusual in this. Instead of being fooled by the Western costume, and instead of being persuaded that he no longer really existed as an Asian, he recognized that the West had something good about it that was good not because it was Western but because it was also Eastern:

that is to say, it was *universal*. So he turned his face and his heart once again to India, and saw what was really there. It was through his acquaintance with writers like Tolstoy and Thoreau, and then his reading of the New Testament, that Gandhi rediscovered his own tradition and his Hindu *dharma* (religion, duty). More than a tradition, more than a wisdom handed down in books or celebrated in temples, Gandhi discovered India in discovering himself. Hence it is very important indeed to understand Gandhi's political life, and particularly his non-violence, in the light of this radical discovery from which everything else received its meaning. Gandhi's dedicated struggle for Indian freedom and his insistence on non-violent means in the struggle—both resulted from his new understanding of India and of himself after his contact with a *universally valid* spiritual tradition which he saw to be common to both East and West.

The Christianity, the spiritual and religious humanism, of the West opened his eyes to forces of wisdom and of love which were closer to his own heart because they were expressed in the symbols and philosophic language of his own people, and they could be used immediately to awaken this sleeping and enslaved people to an awareness of its own identity and of its historic vocation. He neither accepted Christianity nor rejected it; he took all that he found in Christian thought that seemed relevant to him as a Hindu. The rest was, at least for the time being, of merely external interest.

Here was no syncretism and no indifferentism. Gandhi had the deepest respect for Christianity, for Christ and the Gospel. In following his way of *satyagraha** he believed he was following the Law of Christ, and it would be difficult to prove that this belief was entirely mistaken—or that it was in any degree insincere.

One of the great lessons of Gandhi's life remains this: through the spiritual traditions of the West he, an Indian, discovered his Indian heritage and with it his own "right mind." And in his fidelity to his own heritage and its spiritual sanity, he was able to show men of the West and of the whole world a way to recover their own "right mind" in their own tradition, thus manifesting the fact that there are certain indisputable and essential values—religious, ethical, ascetic, spiritual, and philosophical—which man has everywhere needed and which he has in the past managed to acquire, values without which he cannot live, values which are now in large measure lost to him so that, unequipped to face life in a fully human manner, he now runs the risk of destroying himself entirely.

---

*A term coined by Gandhi. Its root meaning is "holding on to truth," and, by extension, resistance by non-violent means.

Call these values what you will, "natural religion" or "natural law," Christianity admits their existence at least as preambles to faith and grace, if not sometimes vastly more (Romans 2:14-15, Acts 17:22-31). These values are universal, and it is hard to see how there can be any "catholicity" (*cath-holos* means "all-embracing") that even implicitly excludes them. One of the marks of catholicity is precisely that values which are everywhere natural to man are fulfilled on the highest level in the Law of the Spirit. And in Christian charity. A "charity" that excludes these values cannot claim the title of Christian love.

In rediscovering India and his own "right mind," Gandhi was not excavating from libraries the obscure disputed questions of Vedantic scholasticism (though he did not reject Vedanta). He was, on the contrary, identifying himself fully with the Indian people, that is to say not with the Westernized upper classes nor with the Brahmin caste, but rather with the starving masses and in particular with the outcaste "untouchables," or *Harijan*.

This again is a supremely important fact, without which Gandhi's nonviolence is incomprehensible. The awakening of the Indian mind in Gandhi was not simply the awakening of his own spirit to the possibilities of a distinctly Hindu form of "interior life." It was not just a question of Yoga *asanas* and Vedantic spiritual disciplines for his own perfection. Gandhi realized that *the people of India were awakening in him*. The masses who had been totally silent for thousands of years had now found a voice in him. It was not "Indian thought" or "Indian spirituality" that was stirring in him, but India herself. It was the spiritual consciousness of a people that awakened in the spirit of one person. But the message of the Indian spirit, of Indian wisdom, was not for India alone. It was for the entire world. Hence Gandhi's message was valid for India and for himself in so far as it represented *the awakening of a new world*.

Yet this renewed spiritual consciousness of India was entirely different from the totalitarian and nationalist consciousnesses that came alive in the West and in the East (Japan) to the point of furious and warlike vitality. The Indian mind that was awakening in Gandhi was inclusive not exclusive. It was at once Indian and universal. It was not a mind of hate, of intolerance, of accusation, of rejection, of division. It was a mind of love, of understanding, of infinite capaciousness. Where the extreme nationalisms of Western Fascism and of Japan were symptoms of paranoid fury, exploding into alienation, division, and destruction, the spirit which Gandhi discovered in himself was reaching out to unity, love, and peace. It was a spirit which was, he believed, strong enough to heal every division.

In Gandhi's mind, non-violence was not simply a political tactic which was supremely useful and efficacious in liberating his people from foreign rule, in order that India might then concentrate on realizing its own national identity. On the contrary, the spirit of non-violence sprang from *an inner realization of spiritual unity in himself*. The whole Gandhian concept of non-violent action and *satyagraha* is incomprehensible if it is thought to be a means of achieving unity rather than as *the fruit of inner unity already achieved*.

Indeed this is the explanation for Gandhi's apparent failure (which became evident to him at the end of his own life). He saw that his followers had not reached the inner unity that he had realized in himself, and that their *satyagraha* was to a great extent a pretense, since they believed it to be a means to achieve unity and freedom, while he saw that it must necessarily be the *fruit of inner freedom*.

The first thing of all and the most important of all was the inner unity, the overcoming and healing of inner division, the consequent spiritual and personal freedom, of which national autonomy and liberty would only be consequences. However, when *satyagraha* was seen only as a useful technique for attaining a pragmatic end, political independence, it remained almost meaningless. As soon as the short-term end was achieved, *satyagraha* was discarded. No inner peace was achieved, no inner unity, only the same divisions, the conflicts and the scandals that were ripping the rest of the world to pieces.

This, then, is the second crucially important principle that we discover in Gandhi. Contrary to what has been thought in recent centuries in the West, the spiritual or interior life is not an exclusively private affair. (In reality, the deepest and most authentic Western traditions are at one with those of the East on this point.) The spiritual life of one person is simply the life of all manifesting itself in him. While it is very necessary to emphasize the truth that as the person deepens his own thought in silence he enters into a deeper understanding of and communion with the spirit of his entire people (or of his Church), it is also important to remember that as he becomes engaged in the crucial struggles of his people, in seeking justice and truth together with his brother, he tends to liberate the truth in himself by seeking true liberty for all. Thus Plato taught that "to philosophize and concern oneself with politics is one and the same thing, and to wrestle with the sophist means at the same time to defend the city against tyranny." (8)

So true was this that Socrates would not turn his back on the equivocation of his fellow citizens and their betrayal of truth, even when their hatred of reason meant his own death.

The "spiritual space" created by the Polis was still, in any event, the only place for the philosopher. True, in an imperfect city a fully human life was not possible, and hence *a fortiori* the perfect philosophical life was out of the question. "The philosopher has no place in the city except at its helm." Yet if he is not only silenced but even condemned unjustly to death, it remains his function as philosopher to teach the city truth by his death rather than fly into exile or withdraw into private life, since a purely private existence could not be fully "philosophical." This was Gandhi's view also, and we know that he had no illusions about the perfection of the Indian Polis.

Gandhi's career was eminently active rather than contemplative. Yet his fidelity in maintaining intact the contemplative element that is necessary in *every* life was well known. However, even his days of silence and retirement were not days of mere "privacy"; they belonged to India and he owed them to India, because his "spiritual life" was simply his participation in the life and *dharma* of his people. Their liberation and the recovery of their political unity would be meaningless unless their liberty and unity had a dimension that was primarily spiritual and religious. The liberation of India was to Gandhi a *religious* duty because for him the liberation of India was only a step to the liberation of all mankind from the tyranny of violence in others, but chiefly in themselves. So Gandhi could say, "When the practice of *ahimsa* becomes universal, God will reign on earth as He does in heaven." (See below, page 25.)

The life of the Indian sage, or guru, is in any case public to the point of being excruciating. Day and night Gandhi was surrounded not only by respect but by worship. Somewhere in *The Human Condition* Hannah Arendt speaks of the Greek citizen's "merciless exposure to the Polis." It was in the life of the Polis that the citizen manifested his deeds and his courage, above all his reason. "No activity can become excellent if the world does not provide a proper space for its exercise." (9)

This does not mean that the classical idea allows no "space" for what is hidden and private. There is the economy of private life in the home. But this is not the proper sphere of man's activities as a being of logic, of courage, and of wisdom. It is in the public and political realm that he shares words and deeds, thus contributing his share of action and thought to the fabric of human affairs. Now, the public and political realm is that where issues are decided in a way worthy of free man: by persuasion and words, not by violence. Violence is essentially wordless, and it can begin only where thought and rational communication have broken down. Any society which is geared for violent action is by that very fact systematically unreasonable and inarticulate. Thought is not encouraged, and the exchange of ideas is eschewed as filled with all manner of risk. Words are kept at a minimum, at least as far as their variety and content may be concerned, though they may pour over the armed multitude in cataracts: they are simply organized and inarticulate noise destined to arrest thought and release violence, inhibiting all desire to communicate with the enemy in any other way than by destructive impact.

Though there are at best only analogies between the Greek concept of the Polis and the entirely hierarchical structure of ancient Indian society, it is instructive to see how these basic ideas are illustrated in Gandhi. It cannot too often be repeated that with him non-violence was not a simply marginal and quasi-fanatical indulgence of personal religious feeling. It belonged to the *very nature of political life,* and a society whose politics are habitually violent, inarticulate, and unreasonable is a subpolitical and therefore subhuman society. This of course was a truth that Gandhi had learned not from books but from experience—in South Africa!

In any case Gandhi's public life was one of maximum exposure, and he kept it so. *For him the public realm was not secular, it was sacred.* To be involved in it was then to be involved in the sacred *dharma* of the Indian people. Surrender to the demands of that *dharma,* to the sacred needs of the *Harijan* (outcastes, untouchables) and of all India, was purely and simply surrender to God and to His will, manifested in the midst of the people. When friends tried to dissuade Gandhi from fasting for the people (and Gandhi's fasts were completely public, political acts in the highest sense of the word) he replied: "God's voice has been increasingly audible as years have rolled by. He has never forsaken me even in my darkest hour. He has saved me often against myself and left me not a vestige of independence. The greater the surrender to Him, the greater has been my joy." (10)

Yet it would be a mistake to think of these fasts only as means of applying political (in the lowest and current sense) pressure to achieve short-term ends.

Fasting remained primarily an act of worship and an act of witness to universal truth. It formed part of the Hindu *dharma* and therefore of India's witness to the religious truths implicit in the very structure of cosmic reality. Hence for Gandhi to speak, write, fast, and exercise non-violent resistance in behalf of the *Harijan* and of Indian freedom was at the same time to bear witness to the chief truth of Hinduism: "The belief that ALL life (not only human beings but all sentient beings) is one, i.e., all life coming from the One universal source, call it Allah, God or Parameshwara . . ." (11)

8

Gandhi adds an interesting commentary to this. His immediate conclusion is one that is full of social and moral consequences: "Hinduism excludes all exploitation" (hence it follows implicitly that the caste structure in so far as it rested upon a basis of crass injustice toward the *Harijan* was in fact a denial of the basic truth of Hinduism). Gandhi's sense of the Hindu *dharma* demanded, then, that this be made clear and that all Hindus should collaborate in setting things right. This fundamental re-establishment of justice was essential if India was to have the inner unity, strength, and freedom to profit by its own political liberation.

At the same time, the cooperation of the whole Indian people in the sacrificial and religious art of non-violent self-liberation was a necessary sign to the rest of the world—a witness that would enable all peoples, especially those subject to colonialist exploitation, to take the same measures for the restoration of the order willed by God.

Gandhi continues:

> There is no limit whatsoever to the measure of sacrifice that one may make in order to realize this *oneness with all life,* but certainly the immensity of the ideal sets a limit to your wants. That, you will see, is the antithesis of the position of the modern civilization which says "Increase your wants." Those who hold that belief think that increase of wants means an increase of knowledge whereby you understand the Infinite better. On the contrary, Hinduism rules out indulgence and multiplication of wants, as these hamper one's growth to the ultimate identity with the Universal Self.(12)

Gandhi therefore did not identify the "private" sphere with the "sacred" and did not cut himself off from public activity as "secular." Yet he did on the other hand look upon certain cultures and social structures as basically "secular" in the sense that their most fundamental preconceptions were irreligious (even though they might, on occasion, appeal to the support of religious clichés). Some of the most characteristic and least understood elements in his non-violent mystique follow from this principle which implies a rejection of the basic idea of the affluent industrial society. A society that lives by organized greed or by systematic terrorism and oppression (they come to much the same thing in the end) will always tend to be violent because it is in a state of persistent disorder and moral confusion. The first principle of valid political action in such a society then becomes *non-cooperation* with its disorder, its injustices, and more particularly with its deep commitment to untruth. *Satyagraha* is meaningless if it is not based on the awareness of profound inner contradiction in all societies based on force. "It is not possible for a modern state based on force non-violently to resist forces of disorder, whether external or internal" (see below, page 31). Hence *satyagraha* according to Gandhi cannot seriously accept claims advanced by a basically violent society that hopes to preserve order and peace by the threat of maximum destruction and total hate. *Satyagraha* must begin by putting itself against this claim in order that the seriousness of one's dedication to truth may be put to the test. It is not possible for the truly nonviolent man simply to ignore the inherent falsity and inner contradictions of a violent society. On the contrary, it is for him a religious and human duty to confront the untruth in that society with his own witness in order that the falsity may become evident to everyone. The first job of a *satyagrahi* is to bring the real situation to light even if he has to suffer and die in order that injustice be unmasked and appear for what it really is.

All the political acts of Gandhi were, then, at the same time spiritual and religious acts in fulfillment of the Hindu *dharma*. They were meaningful on at least three different levels at once: first as acts of religious worship, second as symbolic and educative acts bringing the Indian people to a realization of their true needs and their place in the life of the world, and finally they had a universal import as manifestations of urgent truths, the unmasking of political falsehood, awakening all men to the demands of the time and to the need for renewal and unity on a world scale.

In Gandhi the voice of Asia, not the Asia of the Vedas and Sutras only, but the Asia of the hungry and silent masses, was speaking and still speaks to the whole world with a prophetic message. This message, uttered on dusty Indian roads, remains more meaningful than those specious promises that have come from the great capitals of the earth. As Father Monchanin, the French priest and scholar who became a hermit in India, declared at Gandhi's death: "When we hear the voice of Gandhi we hear the voice of his Mother [India] and of his nurse. We hear the voice of all the peasant masses bending over the rice fields of India." (13)

"Man cannot be free if he does not know that he is subject to necessity, because his freedom is always won in his never wholly successful attempts to liberate himself from necessity." (14)

We have seen that Gandhi's political philosophy was based on this principle, because his religious intuition of the Hindu *dharma* saw all life as one in a sacred cosmic family in which each member helped to elevate the whole from a selfish and destructive to a spiritual and productive level through sacrificial participation in the common needs and struggles of all. Hence the cornerstone of all Gandhi's life, action, and thought was the respect for the sacredness of life and the conviction that "love is the law of our being." For he said, "If love or non-violence be not the law of our being, the whole of my argument falls to pieces." (See below, page 25.) Note he also says that "Truth is the law of our being." But obviously Gandhi's life was without meaning unless we take into account the fact that it was lived in the face of untruth and hatred, the persistent and flagrant denial of love.

Sometimes the idea of non-violence is taken to be the result of a purely sentimental evasion of unpleasant reality. Foggy clichés about Oriental metaphysics leave complacent Westerners with the idea that for the East (and as everyone knows, the Easterners are all "quietists" besides being "enigmatic") nothing really exists anyway. All is illusion, and suffering itself is illusion. Non-violence becomes a way of "making violence stop" by sitting down in front of it and wishing it was not there. This, together with the refusal to eat meat or to kill ants, indeed even mosquitoes, is supposedly thought to create an aura of benevolence which may effectively inhibit the violence of Englishmen (who are in any case kind to dogs, etc.) but cannot be expected to work against Nazis and Russians. So much for Western evaluations!

Gandhi knew the reality of hatred and untruth because he had felt them in his own flesh: indeed he succumbed to them when he was assassinated on January 30, 1948. Gandhi's non-violence was therefore not a sentimental evasion or denial of the reality of evil. It was a clearsighted acceptance of the necessity to use the force and the presence of evil as a fulcrum for good and for liberation.

All forms of necessity can contribute to man's freedom. There is material and economic need. There is spiritual need. The greatest of man's spiritual needs is the need to be delivered from the evil and falsity that are in himself and in his society. Tyranny, which makes a sagacious use of every human need and indeed artificially creates more of them in order to exploit them all to the limit, recognizes the importance of guilt. And modern tyrannies have all explicitly or implicitly in one way or another emphasized the *irreversibility of evil* in order to build their power upon it.

For instance, it is not unusual in all political life, whether totalitarian or democratic, to incriminate the political novice in order to test his mettle and make sure of his commitment. He must be willing to get his hands dirty, and if he is not willing he must be framed so that he will have a record that can, when necessary, be used against him. Then he will be a committed man. He will henceforth cooperate with acts which might have given him pause if he were not himself marked with guilt. Who is he to complain of certain shady actions, certain discreet deals, certain white lies, when he knows what is in his own file at headquarters?

It is no accident that Hitler believed firmly in the unforgivableness of sin. This is indeed fundamental to the whole mentality of Nazism, with its avidity for final solutions and its concern that all uncertainties be eliminated.

Hitler's world was built on the central dogma of the irreversibility of evil. Just as there could be no quarter for the Jews, so the acts that eliminated them were equally irreversible and there could really be no excuse for the Nazis themselves. Even the arguments of an Eichmann, pleading obedience, suggest deep faith in an irreversible order which could not be changed but only obeyed. Such was the finality of Hitler's acts and orders that all the trials of all the Nazis who have been caught, whether they have been executed or liberated or put in prison for short terms, have changed absolutely nothing. It is clear that Hitler was in one thing a brilliant success: everything he did bears the stamp of complete and paranoid finality.

In St. Thomas Aquinas, we find a totally different view of evil. Evil is not only reversible but it is the proper motive of that mercy by which it is overcome and changed into good. Replying to the objection that moral evil is not the motive for mercy since the evil of sin deserves indignation and punishment rather than mercy and forgiveness, St. Thomas says that on the contrary *sin itself is already a punishment* "and in this respect we feel sorrow and compassion for sinners." (15) In order to do this we have to be able to *experience their sin as if it were our own*. But those who "consider themselves happy and whose *sense of power depends on the idea that they are beyond suffering any evil* are not able to have mercy on others" by experiencing the evil of others as their own. (16)

This is a splendid analysis of the mentality of power and greed which makes evil irreversible! Such a mentality lacks the interior strength necessary to assume the suffering of another as its own and thus to change his condition by forgiveness and acceptance. Instead of seeing the sin of another as punishment and suffering, and as motive for compassion, it looks on that evil as a despicable moral blemish which must be eliminated and punished, removed from sight and from experience. Only the admission of defect and fallibility in oneself makes it possible for one to become merciful to others.

St. Thomas continues this remarkable analysis by considering those who are "obsessed" with the notion of insult, either because they have suffered a humiliation or because they intend to humiliate another.

They are provoked to anger and aggression, which are virile passions. These make a man think that he is in danger of suffering some future evil (which he intends to resist). When men are so disposed, they do not have mercy on others. Likewise the proud do not have mercy because they despise others and look upon them as evil, taking it for granted that these people deserve to suffer whatever they have to suffer.(17)

A belief in the finality and irreversibility of evil implies a refusal to accept the precariousness and the risk that attend all finite good in this life. Indeed, the good that men do is always in the realm of the uncertain and of the fluid, because the needs and sufferings of men, the sins and failures of men, are constant, and love triumphs, at least in this life, not by eliminating evil once for all but by resisting and overcoming it anew every day. The good is not assured once for all by one heroic act. It must be recaptured over and over again. St. Peter looked for a limit to forgiveness. Seven times, and then the sin was irreversible! But Christ told him that forgiveness must be repeated over and over again, without end.

The "fabric" of society is not finished. It is always "in becoming." It is on the loom, and it is made up of constantly changing relationships. Non-violence takes account precisely of this dynamic and non-final state of all relationships among men, for non-violence seeks to change relationships that are evil into others that are good, or at least less bad.

Hence non-violence implies a kind of bravery far different from violence. In the use of force, one simplifies the situation by assuming that the evil to be overcome is clear-cut, definite, and irreversible. Hence there remains but one thing: to eliminate it. Any dialogue with the sinner, any question of the irreversibility of his act, only means faltering and failure. Failure to eliminate evil is itself a defeat. Anything that even remotely risks such defeat is in itself capitulation to evil. The irreversibility of evil then reaches out to contaminate *even the tolerant thought* of the hesitant crusader who, momentarily, doubts the total evil of the enemy he is about to eliminate.

Such tolerance is already complicity and guilt, and must be eliminated in its turn. As soon as it is detected it becomes irreversible.

Fortitude, then, equals fanaticism. It grows with unreason. Reasoning itself is by its very nature tinged with betrayal.

Conscience does indeed make cowards. It makes Judases. Conscience must be eliminated.

This is the familiar mental machinery of tyrannical oppression. By reducing necessities to simple and irreversible forms it simplifies existence, eliminating questions that tend to embarrass minds and slacken the "progress" of the relentless and intolerant apparatus. Sin is thus prevented from entering into the living dialectic of society. And yet a dialectic that ignores the presence of evil is itself dead because it is untrue. The greatest of tyrannies are all therefore based on the postulate that *there should never be any sin*. That therefore what happened either was not a sin ("Dallas has no sins," as we all were quasi-officially informed at the end of 1963) or else it has been immediately wiped out (by a lynch mob, or a Jack Ruby). Since sin is what should never be, then it must never be, therefore *it will never be*. The most awful tyranny is that of the proximate Utopia where the last sins are currently being eliminated and where, tomorrow, there will be no more sins because all the sinners will have been wiped out.

> Non-violence has a different logic. It recognizes that sin is an everyday occurrence which is in the very nature of action's constant establishment of new relationships within a web of relations, and it needs forgiving, dismissing, in order to make it possible for life to go on by constantly releasing men from what they have done unknowingly. Only through this constant mutual release from what they do can men remain free agents, only by their constant willingness to change their minds and start again can they be trusted with so great a power as that to begin something new. (18)

This remarkable statement of Hannah Arendt's shows the inherent relation between non-violence and the renewal of India for which Gandhi lived and died. A violent change would not have been a serious change at all. To punish and destroy the oppressor is merely to initiate a new cycle of violence and oppression. The only real liberation is that which *liberates both the oppressor and the oppressed* at the same time from the same tyrannical automatism of the violent process which contains in itself the curse of irreversibility. "The freedom contained in Jesus' teaching of forgiveness is the *freedom from vengeance,* [italics mine] which encloses both doer and sufferer in the relentless automatism of the action process, which by itself need never come to an end." (19)

True freedom is then inseparable from the inner strength which can assume the common burden of evil which weighs both on oneself and one's adversary. False freedom is only a manifestation of the weakness that cannot bear even one's own evil until it is projected onto the other and seen as exclusively his. The highest form of spiritual freedom is, as Gandhi believed, to be sought in the strength of heart which is capable of liberating the oppressed and the oppressor together. But in any event, the oppressed must be able to be free within himself, so that he may begin to gain strength to pity his oppressor. Without that capacity for pity, neither of them will be able to recognize the truth of their situation: a common relationship in a common complex of sins.

When asked if it was lawful to overcome force with force, Erasmus answered that this might be permissible according to "Imperial laws" but he wondered how it could be relevant for a Christian, who is bound to follow the law of Christ,

> granted that human laws do not punish what they have permitted. Yet what is Christ your leader going to do if you defraud this law . . . If your enemy is hungry, give him to eat . . . In so doing you will heap coals of fire upon his head, that is to say, you will enkindle the fire of love in him.

To the objection that rendering good for evil only lays one open to greater evil, Erasmus replied:

> If you can avoid evil by suffering it yourself, do so. Try to help your enemy by overcoming him with kindness and meekness. If this does not help, then it is better that one perish than both of you. It is better that you be enriched with the advantage of patience than to render evil for evil. It is not enough to practice the golden rule in this matter. The greater your position the more ready you ought to be to forgive another's crime. (20)

Here, as usual in Erasmus, one finds no platitudes. The apparently simple suggestion that one can avoid evil by suffering it contains an arresting paradox. One can overcome evil by taking it upon oneself, whereas if one flies from it he is not certain to escape and may, even if he seems to escape, be overwhelmed. The only way truly to "overcome" an enemy is to help him become other than an enemy. This is the kind of wisdom we find in Gandhi. It is the wisdom of the Gospels.

It is also the wisdom of the Apostolic Fathers. We read in the *Shepherd of Hermas*:

> For, if you are long-suffering, the Holy Spirit dwelling in you will be clear, unobscured by any other spirit of evil. Dwelling in a spacious place, He will rejoice and be glad with the lodging in which He finds Himself. Thus, He will serve God with abundant cheerfulness, because He has His well-being within Himself. However, if violent anger enters, the good spirit in

His sensitiveness is immediately confined, since He has not a clean habitation. So, He tries to withdraw from the place. . . . For, the Lord dwells amid long-suffering, but the Devil has his abode in anger. . . . Take a little wormwood and pour it into a jar of honey. Is not the honey spoiled altogether? Even a great quantity of honey is ruined by the smallest amount of wormwood and its sweetness is lost. It is no longer pleasant to the owner, because it has been mixed and it is no longer enjoyable. Now, if no wormwood is put into the honey, it turns out to be sweet and becomes useful for the owner. You see, then, that long-suffering is very sweet, far more than honey, and useful to the Lord. His dwelling is in long-suffering. (21)

Gandhi took upon himself the evil of India, not in a spirit of masochism or with the spiritual frivolity of self-punishment that believes itself to have a magic efficacy over sin. Nothing is more deeply serious than the Gandhian fast unto death for the recognition of the *Harijan* and for their admission to the temple, in a word their integration into the sacred public life of the Indian people.

He did not seek to reproach and confound others with the spectacle of his own penitence for their sin. He wanted them to recognize from his example that they could learn to bear and overcome the evil that was in them if they were willing to do as he did. Gandhi's symbolic acts (which were meaningful as symbols only because they marked his own flesh with the stamp of their acute reality) were aimed at three kinds of liberation. First, he wanted to deliver Indian religious wisdom from the sclerosis and blindness into which it had sunk by reason of the gross injustices of a system which had become untrue to itself. Second, he wanted to liberate the untouchables, the *Harijan*, not only from political and economic oppression, but from the incubus of their own self-hate and their despair. And, finally, he wished to liberate the oppressors themselves from their blind and hopeless dependence on the system which kept things as they were, and which consequently enslaved everybody both spiritually and materially.

What is most striking in this concept of Gandhi's is its breadth, its integrity, and its unity. This is his lesson and his legacy to the world: The evils we suffer cannot be eliminated by a violent attack in which one sector of humanity flies at another in destructive fury. Our evils are common and the solution of them can only be common. But we are not ready to undertake this common task because we are not ourselves. Consequently the first duty of every man is to return to his own "right mind" in order that society itself may be sane.

Coomaraswamy, in an important article (22), once outlined the meaning of the process called *metanoia,* or recovery of one's right mind, the passage from ignorance of self to enlightened moral awareness. "Repentance," he said, quoting Hermas (23), "is a great understanding" (and by no means an emotional crisis!). It is the ability to cast off the intolerable burden of the past act, no longer seen as irreversible. But obviously no man enclosed in himself can utter an omnipotent word of command and abolish his own sin. The "knowledge" and "understanding" which is truly the "great [and repentant, liberated] understanding" is therefore "understanding-with" or "*con*-scientia" (conscience). "A kind of synthesis or agreement by which our internal conflict is resolved and 'all the knots of the heart are loosed.'" It is to understand "with" our inmost self "*in a union transcending consciousness of a within or a without.*"

This is obviously something much deeper than a mere interiority or a form of pious and introverted recollection. It is supraconscious and suprapersonal. And it obviously implies the ability to come into unity with the *prajnatman* (the solar spirit), or what the Greek Fathers would call the *pneuma.*

We find St. Thomas speaking somewhat in these terms in an interesting question in the *Summa* on blindness of mind.(24) There is, he says, a principle of intellectual vision in man, and man can give his attention to this principle or turn away from it. He turns away either by willful refusal to acknowledge its authority, or by becoming absorbed in the love of other things which he prefers to the intellectual light. And St. Thomas quotes Psalm 57:9—*Fire hath fallen on them* (the fire of desire) *and they shall not see the sun.*

The *Shepherd of Hermas* speaks of the Spirit of Truth as a trust given by God to man, living and dwelling in him in order to be returned to the Lord undefiled by any lie. "Love truth and let nothing but the truth issue from your mouth, in order that the spirit which God has settled in this flesh of yours may be found truthful in the sight of men. . . . Liars ignore the Lord and defraud Him since they do not return the Spirit received from Him, namely a Spirit in which there is no lie." Hearing this, Hermas weeps and declares: "I have not yet spoken a true word in all my life!" And the Angel then tells him that this declaration is the beginning of truth in himself.(25) Of course in this context truth and forgiveness go together, and there must be *one* truth and one forgiveness both for myself and my brothers. Both truth and mercy are falsified when I judge by a double standard.

The capacity for forgiveness and for understanding in this highest sense makes men able to transcend the limitations of that self which is the subject of evil. St. Cyprian says, "If no one can be without sin . . . how necessary and how beneficent is divine clemency which, since it recognizes that even those who are healed still retain some wounds, has granted health-giving remedies to be used in curing the wounds that remain to be healed." (26) But this is not a merely mental operation, a manipulation of "pure intentions" and the excitation of subjective benevolence toward offenders. It means an immolation of one's empirical self, by mercy and sacrifice, in order to save and liberate oneself and the other. Coomaraswamy here quotes the *Maitri Upanishad*: "When the mind has been immolated in its own source for love of truth, THEN THE FALSE CONTROLS OF ACTIONS DONE WHEN IT WAS DELUDED BY SENSIBILIA LIKEWISE PASS AWAY." This is the mystical basis of Gandhi's doctrine of freedom in truth as end, and of *satyagraha* (the vow of truth) as the means of attaining the end. Coomaraswamy also quotes a few lines from Jakob Boehme which throw light on this idea which is, of course, fundamentally Christian. Boehme says:

> Thou shalt do nothing but forsake thy own will, viz., that which thou callest "I" or "thyself." By which means all thy evil properties will grow weak, faint and ready to die, then thou wilt sink down again into that one thing from which thou art originally sprung.

To forgive others and to forget their offense is to enter with them into the healing mystery of death and resurrection in Christ, to return to the source of the Spirit which is the Heart of Christ. And by this forgiveness we are ourselves cleansed: *Unde vulneratus fueras, inde curare,* says Cyprian. (27)

It should be quite obvious that *satyagraha* has nothing in it of Western middle-class banality. It does not mean "honesty is the best policy," because it is far more than honesty and it is infinitely more than a policy. One does not obey the *prajnatman,* or intellectual principle, the "spirit of truth," simply in order to get something out of one's obedience.

The truth may turn out in terms of the current moods and trends of a blind society to be supremely unprofitable. In that case, when truth becomes absolutely the worst policy, one follows it anyway, even when it leads to death.

The "vivisection" of liberated India into two hostile states was in fact the rending of Gandhi's own heart. Though India was technically "free," it was not free because it was not united. It was indeed placed in a situation of mortal danger, in which the perpetual threat of violence made true freedom and true unity impossible.

It remained for Gandhi to start all over again as a solitary. "The interior voice tells me to go on fighting against the whole world, even though I am alone. It tells me not to fear this world but to advance, having in myself nothing but the fear of God." At the same time he did not give up hope for India, because the truth of the Hindu *dharma* remained what it had always been, and if India wished to fulfill the conditions of fidelity to her *dharma,* she could recover this truth.

"A man ends by becoming what he thinks," Gandhi said, "and it will be the same for India if she remains firmly attached to Truth by means of Love [*satyagraha*]." But he himself recognized that politically his battle had really been lost. Without complacency, without self-pity, he faced the truth that there was only one thing left. He must lay down his life for India, and he was in fact killed by a brother "whom he had failed to convince."

Whether we may think he succeeded or failed, Gandhi never ceased to believe in the possibility of a love of truth so strong and so pure that it would leave an "indelible impress" upon the most recalcitrant enemy, and awaken in him a response of love and truth. Such an attitude cannot be understood within the context of pragmatism, because what matters is the devotion to truth which it implies, not its actual impact on other men.

In retrospect one wonders how deeply India herself understood Gandhi and believed in him. Tagore himself, one of the greatest Indian minds of our time, doubted the Mahatma and leveled against him the accusation with which we are all too familiar in the West. "Non-cooperation" (with the British) seemed to Tagore to be nothing but negation, defeatism, passivity, and so on. The standard and lasting objection to Gandhi has always been that he was retreating into the past. He is accused of not seeing that there was no alternative for India but acceptance of the values and methods of the West with all their implications, including the rejection of what was most fundamentally and characteristically Eastern.

Thus, for Tagore, the refusal to attend English Government schools (suggested by Gandhi) was nothing more than a withdrawal into a kind of Hindu ghetto. One should do all one possibly could to acquire the techniques and attitudes of Western man, and then turn these against the oppressor. This has been the formula adopted wholeheartedly, for example, by Communist China.

Gandhi's idea was quite different. "Non-cooperation," he declared, "is a protest against an unwitting and unwilling participation in evil." The institutions of colonialism were in reality not intended to elevate and liberate the Indian. On the contrary, "the Government schools have unmanned us, rendered us helpless and Godless. They have filled us with discontent, and providing no remedy for the discontent have made us despondent. They have made us what we were intended to become: clerks and interpreters." (28)

How clear this has since become in the predicament of the new nations of Asia and Africa, suddenly liberated from colonial tutelage! Having accepted the white man's "culture" in their status as vassals, and still remaining intellectual and spiritual vassals after their liberation, they have entered a world of frustration, self-contradiction, resentment, and violence because the guilt of the colonial powers has been inherited, by them, as a tenfold self-hate, an incapacity to understand themselves, and a limitless fear and suspicion of everyone else. This is neither liberty nor civilization. It is the barbarism of post-historic man! A barbarism that can be avoided only by principles and policies like those of Gandhi or John XXIII.

Gandhi knew enough to see that to be "civilized" by force was in reality to be reduced oneself to barbarism, while the "civilizer" himself was barbarized. Can anyone deny that this has happened?

In conclusion, Gandhi's "vow of truth" and all the other *ashram* vows, which were the *necessary preamble to the awakening of a mature political consciousness,* must be seen for what they are: not simply ascetic or devotional indulgences that may possibly suit the fancy of a few religious pacifists and confused poets, but precepts fundamentally necessary if man is to recover his right mind.

Gandhi's principles are, then, extremely pertinent today, more pertinent even than when they were conceived and worked out in practice in the *ashrams,* villages, and highways of India. They are pertinent for everybody, but especially for those who are interested in implementing the principles expressed by another great religious mind, Pope John XXIII, in *Pacem in Terris.* Indeed this encyclical has the breadth and depth, the universality and tolerance, of Gandhi's own peace-minded outlook. Peace cannot be built on exclusivism, absolutism, and intolerance. But neither can it be built on vague liberal slogans and pious programs gestated in the smoke of confabulation. There can be no peace on earth without the kind of inner change that brings man back to his "right mind."

Gandhi's observations on the prerequisites and the disciplines involved by *satyagraha,* the vow of truth, are required reading for anyone who is seriously interested in man's fate in the nuclear age.

THOMAS MERTON

Abbey of Gethsemani
April, 1964.

SELECTIONS FROM

GANDHI'S

Non-Violence in Peace and War

SECTION ONE

Principles of Non-Violence

Ahimsa (non-violence) is for Gandhi the basic law of our being. That is why it can be used as the most effective principle for social action, since it is in deep accord with the truth of man's nature and corresponds to his innate desire for peace, justice, order, freedom, and personal dignity. Since *himsa* (violence) degrades and corrupts man, to meet force with force and hatred with hatred only increases man's progressive degeneration. Non-violence, on the contrary, heals and restores man's nature, while giving him a means to restore social order and justice. *Ahimsa* is not a policy for the seizure of power. It is a way of transforming relationships so as to bring about a peaceful transfer of power, effected freely and without compulsion by all concerned, because all have come to recognize it as right.

Since *ahimsa* is in man's nature itself, it can be learned by all, though Gandhi is careful to state that he does not expect everyone to practice it perfectly. However, all men should be willing to engage in the risk and wager of *ahimsa* because violent policies have not only proved bankrupt but threaten man with extinction.

There is no half way between truth and non-violence on the one hand and untruth and violence on the other. We may never be strong enough to be entirely non-violent in thought, word and deed. But we must keep non-violence as our goal and make steady progress towards it. The attainment of freedom, whether for a man, a nation or the world, must be in exact proportion to the attainment of non-violence by each.   I – 58*

Non-violence is not a garment to be put on and off at will. Its seat is in the heart, and it must be an inseparable part of our very being.   I – 61

The acquisition of the spirit of non-resistance is a matter of long training in self-denial and appreciation of the hidden forces within ourselves. It changes one's outlook on life. . . . It is the greatest force because it is the highest expression of the soul.   I – 63

If one is to combat the fetish of force, it will only be by means totally different from those in vogue among the pure worshippers of brute force.   I – 65

Principles

Non-violence implies as complete self-purification as is humanly possible.

Man for man the strength of non-violence is in exact proportion to the ability, not the will, of the non-violent person to inflict violence.

The power at the disposal of a non-violent person is always greater than he would have if he were violent.

There is no such thing as defeat in non-violence.   I – 111

*References throughout are to the two-volume edition of *Non-Violence in Peace and War*, published by Navajivan Publishing House, Ahmedabad, 1948.

Ahimsa (non-violence)
  It is the only true force in life.   I – 114

This is the only permanent thing in life, this is the only thing that counts; whatever effort you bestow on mastering it is well spent. I – 114

If love or non-violence be not the law of our being, the whole of my argument falls to pieces.   I – 121

When the practice of *ahimsa* becomes universal, God will reign on earth as He does in heaven.   I – 121

I know this cannot be proved by argument. It shall be proved by persons living it in their lives with utter disregard of consequences to themselves.   I – 122

Given the proper training and proper generalship, non-violence can be practiced by the masses of mankind.   I – 168

Non-violence is the supreme law. During my half a century of experience I have not yet come across a situation when I had to say that I was helpless, that I had no remedy in terms of non-violence.   I – 172

Belief in non-violence is based on the assumption that human nature in its essence is one and therefore unfailingly responds to the advances of love. . . . The non-violent technique does not depend for its success on the goodwill of the dictators, for a non-violent resister depends on the unfailing assistance of God which sustains him throughout difficulties which would otherwise be considered insurmountable.   I – 175

Jesus lived and died in vain if He did not teach us to regulate the whole of life by the eternal law of love.   I – 181

If one does not practice non-violence in one's personal relations with others and hopes to use it in bigger affairs, one is vastly mistaken. . . . Mutual forbearance is not non-violence. Immediately you get the conviction that non-violence is the law of life, you have to practice it towards those who act violently towards you; and the law must apply to nations as to individuals. If the conviction is there, the rest will follow.   I – 187

My optimism rests on my belief in the infinite possibilities of the individual to develop non-violence. The more you develop it in your own being, the more infectious it becomes till it overwhelms your surroundings and by and by might oversweep the world.   I – 190

The Congress can remain non-communal only if it becomes truly non-violent in all matters. It cannot be non-violent only towards the rulers and violent towards others. That way lie disgrace and disaster.   I – 261

I believe that a state can be administered on a non-violent basis if the vast majority of the people are non-violent. So far as I know, India is the only country which has a possibility of being such a state. I am conducting my experiment in that faith.   I – 265

[In non-violence] the bravery consists in dying, not in killing.   I – 265

For me non-violence is a creed. I must act up to it whether I am alone or have companions. Since propaganda of non-violence is the mission of my life, I must pursue it in all weathers.   I – 275

Non-violence, which is a quality of the heart, cannot come by an appeal to the brain.   I – 276

I claim to be a passionate seeker after truth, which is but another name for God. In the course of that search the discovery of non-violence came to me. Its spread is my life mission. I have no interest in living except for the prosecution of that mission.   I – 282

There will never be an army of perfectly non-violent people. It will be formed of those who will honestly endeavor to observe non-violence.   I – 300

Those who are attracted to non-violence should, according to their ability and opportunity, join the experiment.   I – 307

Man as animal is violent but as spirit is non-violent. The moment he awakes to the spirit within he cannot remain violent. Either he progresses towards *ahimsa* or rushes to his doom.   I – 311

Imperfect as I am, I started with imperfect men and women and sailed on an uncharted ocean.   I – 396

In the empire of non-violence every true thought counts, every true voice has its full value.   I – 399

I claim to be a votary of truth from my childhood. It was the most natural thing to me. My prayerful search gave me the revealing maxim "Truth is God" instead of the usual one, "God is Truth." That maxim enables me to see God face to face as it were. I feel Him pervade every fiber of my being. I – 414

A non-violent revolution is not a program of seizure of power. It is a program of transformation of relationships, ending in a peaceful transfer of power. II – 8

Prayer from the heart can achieve what nothing else can in the world. II – 19

In *satyagraha* the cause has to be just and clear as well as the means. II – 33

The ideal of *satyagraha* is not meant for the select few—the saint and the seer only; it is meant for all. II – 34

The true soldier of India is he who spins to clothe the naked and tills the soil to grow more food to meet the threatening food crisis. II – 35

To me it is a self-evident truth that if freedom is to be shared equally by all—even physically the weakest, the lame and the halt—they must be able to contribute an equal share in its defense. How that can be possible when reliance is placed on armaments, my plebian mind fails to understand. I therefore swear and shall continue to swear by non-violence, i.e., by *satyagraha*, or soul force. In it physical incapacity is no handicap, and even a frail woman or a child can pit herself or himself on equal terms against a giant armed with the most powerful weapons. II – 35

In non-violence the masses have a weapon which enables a child, a woman, or even a decrepit old man to resist the mightiest government successfully. If your spirit is strong, mere lack of physical strength ceases to be a handicap.   II – 41

No man has ever been able to describe God fully. The same is true of *ahimsa*.   II – 45

The first principle of non-violent action is that of non-cooperation with everything humiliating.   II – 53

One has to speak out and stand up for one's convictions. Inaction at a time of conflagration is inexcusable.   II – 56

To lay down one's life for what one considers to be right is the very core of *satyagraha*.   II – 59

The sword of the *satyagrahi* is love, and the unshakable firmness that comes from it.   II – 59

The training of *satyagraha* is meant for all, irrespective of age or sex. The more important part of the training here is mental, not physical. There can be no compulsion in mental training.   II – 60

Satyagraha is always superior to armed resistance. This can only be effectively proved by demonstration, not by argument. . . . *Satyagraha* can never be used to defend a wrong cause.   II – 60

Satyagraha is a process of educating public opinion such that it covers all the elements of society and in the end makes itself irresistible.   II – 61

The conditions necessary for the success of *satyagraha* are:
1) The *satyagrahi* should not have any hatred in his heart against the opponent.
2) The issue must be true and substantial.
3) The *satyagrahi* must be prepared to suffer till the end.   II – 61

The root of *satyagraha* is in prayer. A *satyagrahi* relies upon God for protection against the tyranny of brute force.   II – 62

The art of dying for a *satyagrahi* consists in facing death cheerfully in the performance of one's duty.   II – 63

It is a bad outlook for the world if the spirit of violence takes hold of the mass mind. Ultimately it destroys the race.   II – 75

[Moral] practice has not been able to keep pace with the mind. Man has begun to say, "This is wrong, that is wrong." Whereas previously he justified his conduct, he now no longer justifies his own or his neighbor's. He wants to set right the wrong but does not know that his own practice fails him. The contradiction between his thought and conduct fetters him.   II – 76

Non-violence will prevail—whatever man may or may not do. . . . It will have its way and overcome all obstacles irrespective of the shortcomings of the instruments.   II – 76

Prayer is the first and the last lesson in learning the noble and brave art of sacrificing self in the various walks of life culminating in the defense of one's nation's liberty and honor.　　　　II – 77

Undoubtedly prayer requires a living faith in God. Successful *satyagraha* is inconceivable without that faith. God may be called by any other name so long as it connotes the living Law of Life—in other words, the Law and the Lawgiver rolled into one.　　　　II – 78

The virtues of mercy, non-violence, love and truth in any man can be truly tested only when they are pitted against ruthlessness, violence, hate and untruth.　　　　II – 85

The independence of my dreams means *Ramarajya,* i.e., the Kingdom of God on earth. . . . The independence should be political, economic and moral. "Political" means the removal of the control of the British army. "Economic" means entire freedom from British capitalists and capital, as also from their Indian counterparts. "Moral" means freedom from armed defense forces.　　　　II – 88

It is not possible for a modern state based on force non-violently to resist forces of disorder, whether external or internal. A man cannot serve God and Mammon, nor be temperate and furious at the same time.　　II – 90

A non-violent state must be broad-based on the will of an intelligent people well able to know its mind and act up to it.　　　　II – 91

No man can stop violence. God alone can do so. Men are but instruments in His hands. . . . The deciding factor is God's grace. He works according to His law and therefore violence will also be stopped in accordance with that law. Man does not and can never know God's law fully. Therefore we have to try as far as lies in our power. II – 95

Ahimsa is one of the world's great principles which no force on earth can wipe out. Thousands like myself may die in trying to vindicate the ideal, but *ahimsa* will never die. And the gospel of *ahimsa* can be spread only through believers dying for the cause. II – 96

It has been suggested by American friends that the atom bomb will bring in *ahimsa* as nothing else can. . . . This is very like a man glutting himself with dainties to the point of nausea and turning away from them only to return with redoubled zeal after the effect of nausea is well over. Precisely in the same manner will the world return to violence with renewed zeal after the effect of disgust is worn out. II – 96

So far as I can see, the atomic bomb has deadened the finest feeling that has sustained mankind for ages. There used to be the so-called laws of war which made it tolerable. Now we know the naked truth. War knows no law except that of might. The atom bomb brought an empty victory to the allied arms, but it resulted for the time being in destroying the soul of Japan. What has happened to the soul of the destroying nation is yet too early to see. II – 96

Mankind has to get out of violence only through non-violence. Hatred can be overcome only by love. Counter-hatred only increases the surface as well as the depth of hatred. II – 97

I regard the employment of the atom bomb for the wholesale destruction of men, women and children as the most diabolical use of science. II – 98

32

Non-violence is the only thing the atom bomb cannot destroy. . . . Unless now the world adopts non-violence, it will spell certain suicide for mankind.   II – 98

Non-violent defense neither knows nor accepts defeat at any stage. Therefore a nation or a group which has made non-violence its final policy cannot be subjected to slavery even by the atom bomb.   II – 141

A non-violent man or woman will and should die without retaliation, anger or malice, in self-defense or in defending the honor of his women folk. This is the highest form of bravery. If an individual or group of people are unable or unwilling to follow this great law of life, retaliation or resistance unto death is the second best, though a long way off from the first. Cowardice is impotence worse than violence. The coward desires revenge but being afraid to die, he looks to others, maybe to the government of the day, to do the work of defense for him. A coward is less than a man. He does not deserve to be a member of a society of men and women.   II – 148

Satyagraha is never vindictive. It believes not in destruction but in conversion. Its failures are due to the weaknesses of the *satyagrahi,* not to any defect in the law itself.   II – 149

Where there is *ahimsa* there is Truth and Truth is God. How He manifests Himself I cannot say. All I know is that He is all-pervading and where He is all is well.   II – 151

Truth never damages a cause that is just.   II – 162

Unless big nations shed their desire of exploitation and the spirit of violence, of which war is the natural expression and the atom bomb the inevitable consequence, there is no hope for peace in the world.　II – 163

[Jesus—] a man who was completely innocent, offered himself as a sacrifice for the good of others, including his enemies, and became the ransom of the world. It was a perfect act.　II – 166

Goodness must be joined with knowledge. Mere goodness is not of much use, as I have found in life. One must cultivate the fine discriminating quality which goes with spiritual courage and character.　II – 195

The people of Europe are sure to perish if they continue to be violent.
II – 200

God alone knows the mind of a person; and the duty of a man of God is to act as he is directed by his inner voice. I claim that I act accordingly.
II – 204

I ask nobody to follow me. Everyone should follow his own inner voice.　II – 205

If we knew the use of non-violent resistance which only those with hearts of oak can offer, we would present to the world a totally different picture of a free India instead of an India cut in twain.　II – 281

No man, if he is pure, has anything more precious to give than his life.　II – 349

SECTION TWO

Non-Violence: True and False

In this section we have statements which clearly distinguish between the non-violence (*ahimsa*) of the strong and that of the weak. True non-violence not only implies the highest form of bravery: it is a kind of charismatic gift, a "creed" and a "passion," for which one sacrifices everything: it is a complete way of life, in which the *satyagrahi** is totally dedicated to the transformation of his own life, of his adversary, and of society by means of love.

The non-violence of the weak is rather a policy of passive protest, or even a cloak for impotent hatred which does not dare to use force. It is without love. It seeks to harm the adversary in ways that do not involve force, and it may resort to secret sabotage or even terrorism. Such conduct is not worthy of the name of non-violence. It is demoralizing and destructive.

To this false and cowardly non-violence Gandhi says he would prefer an honest resort to force. Hence those who cannot practice a really dedicated non-violence should defend their rights and justice by force, if no other means are available. Gandhi does not preach the passive surrender of rights or of human dignity. On the contrary, he believes that non-violence is the noblest as well as the most effective way of defending one's rights.

Jesus is presented as the model of non-violent resistance.

---

*A *satyagrahi* is one who is consecrated to non-violent defense of the truth.

Non-violence is not a cover for cowardice, but it is the supreme virtue of the brave. . . . Cowardice is wholly inconsistent with non-violence. . . . Non-violence presupposes ability to strike.   I – 59

He who cannot protect himself or his nearest and dearest or their honor by non-violently facing death, may and ought to do so by violently dealing with the oppressor. He who can do neither of the two is a burden.   I – 77

One who having retaliation in his breast submits to violence out of policy is not truly non-violent, and may even be a hypocrite if he hides his intention. It should be remembered that non-violence comes into play only when it comes in contact with violence.   I – 99

Without a direct active expression of it, non-violence, to my mind, is meaningless.   I – 113

[*Non-violence and pride*] If one has pride and egoism, there is no non-violence. Non-violence is impossible without humility. My own experience is that whenever I have acted non-violently I have been led to it and sustained in it by the higher promptings of an unseen power. Through my own will I should have miserably failed.   I – 187

[To a Chinese—1939—re Japan.] In a position of hopeless minority [i.e., the non-violent are very few] you may not ask your people to lay down their arms unless their hearts are changed and by laying down their arms they feel the more courageous and brave. But while you may not try to wean people from war, you will in your person live non-violence in all its completeness and refuse all participation in war. You will develop love for the Japanese in your hearts. . . . You must be able to love them in spite of all their misdeeds. If you have that love for the Japanese in your hearts, you will proceed to exhibit in your conduct that higher form of courage which is the true hallmark of non-violence.   I – 189

[To Chinese Christians in 1939.] If China wins, you will go to the gallows in the attempt to wean China from copying Japan's methods.
I – 192

It is better to be violent, if there is violence in our hearts, than to put on the cloak of non-violence to cover impotence. Violence is any day preferable to impotence. There is hope for a violent man to become non-violent. There is no such hope for the impotent.   I – 240

Ahimsa is an attribute of the brave. Cowardice and *ahimsa* do not go together any more than water and fire.   I – 243

I want the non-violence of the weak [many] to become the non-violence of the brave. It may be a dream, but I have to strive for its realization.
I – 245

[*Hijrat*—self-imposed exile] My advice to migrate is for all who feel oppressed and cannot live without losing self-respect in a particular place. . . . My advice is meant for those who, though they are conscious of self-respect, lack the strength that comes from non-violence or the capacity to return blow for blow.   I – 255

If the capacity for non-violent self-defense is lacking, there need be no hesitation in using violent means. I – 260

War is an unmitigated evil. But it certainly does one good thing. It drives away fear and brings bravery to the surface. I – 270

Non-violence of the strong cannot be a mere policy. It must be a creed, or a passion. . . . A man with a passion expresses it in every little act of his. Therefore he who is possessed by non-violence will express it in the family circle, in his dealings with neighbors, in his business . . . in his dealings with opponents. [Because the Congress members did not show this in their lives it was rightly concluded that they were not ready for non-violence.] I – 276

In *ahimsa* it is not the votary who acts in his own strength. Strength comes from God. . . . Never have I attributed any independent strength to myself. I – 321

The votary of non-violence has to cultivate his capacity for sacrifice of the highest type in order to be free from fear. . . . He who has not overcome all fear cannot practice *ahimsa* to perfection. The votary of *ahimsa* has only one fear, that is of God. He who seeks refuge in God ought to have a glimpse of the *Atman* [the transcendent self] that transcends the body; and the moment one has glimpsed the imperishable *Atman* one sheds the love of the perishable body. . . . Violence is needed for the protection of things external; non-violence is needed for the protection of the *Atman,* for the protection of one's honor. I – 335

We should learn to dare danger and death, mortify the flesh, and acquire the capacity to endure all manner of hardships. I – 335

It is likely that what we believe to be an act of *ahimsa* (non-violence) is an act of *himsa* (violence) in the eyes of God.   I – 338

Non-violence that merely offers civil resistance to the authorities and goes no further scarcely deserves the name *ahimsa*. You may, if you like, call it unarmed resistance. . . . To quell riots non-violently there must be true *ahimsa* in one's heart, an *ahimsa* that takes even the erring hooligan in its warm embrace. Such an attitude cannot be cultivated. It can only come as a prolonged and patient effort which must be made during peaceful times. The would-be member of a peace brigade should come into close touch and cultivate acquaintance with the so-called *goonda* [hooligan] element in his vicinity. He should know and be known to all and win the hearts of all by his living and selfless service. No section should be regarded as too contemptible or mean to mix with. *Goondas* do not drop from the sky, nor do they spring from the earth like evil spirits. They are the product of social disorganization, and society is therefore responsible for their existence. . . . Let everyone who is interested in removing this disease make a prompt beginning in his own neighborhood.   I – 344

[Injustice must be resisted.] No doubt the non-violent way is always the best, but where that does not come naturally the violent way is both necessary and honorable. Inaction here is rank cowardice and unmanly. It must be shunned at all cost.   I – 402

Sabotage is a form of violence. People have realized the futility of physical violence but some people apparently think that it may be successfully practiced in its modified form as sabotage. It is my conviction that the whole mass of people would not have risen to the height of courage and fearlessness that they have but for the working of full non-violence. How it works we do not yet fully know. But the fact remains that under non-violence we have progressed from strength to strength even through our apparent failures and setbacks. On the other hand terrorism resulted in demoralization. Haste leads to waste.   II – 2

No secret organization, however big, could do any good. Secrecy aims at building a wall of protection around you. *Ahimsa* disdains all such protection. It functions in the open in the face of odds, the heaviest conceivable. We have to organize for action a vast people that have been crushed under the heel of unspeakable tyranny for centuries. They cannot be organized by other than open, truthful means. I have grown up from youth to seventy-six years in abhorrence of secrecy. There must be no watering down of the ideal.   II – 2

On India rests the burden of pointing the way to all the exploited races. She won't be able to bear that burden if non-violence does not permeate us more than today. . . . India will become a torch bearer to the oppressed only if she can vindicate the principle of non-violence in her own case, not jettison it as soon as independence of foreign control is achieved.
II – 13

Jesus was the most active resister known perhaps to history. This was non-violence par excellence.   II – 16

Non-violence in the sense of mere non-killing does not appear to me to be any improvement on the technique of violence. It means slow torture, and when slowness becomes ineffective we shall immediately revert to killing and to the atom bomb.   II – 29

So long as one wants to retain one's sword, one has not attained complete fearlessness.   II – 38

A *satyagrahi* may never run away from danger, irrespective of whether he is alone or in the company of many. He will have fully performed his duty if he dies fighting.   II – 59

In life it is impossible to eschew violence completely. The question arises, Where is one to draw the line? The line cannot be the same for everyone. . . . Meat-eating is a sin for me. Yet for another person who has always lived on meat and never seen anything wrong in it, to give it up simply to copy me will be a sin.   II – 69

To allow crops to be eaten up by animals in the name of *ahimsa* while there is a famine in the land is certainly a sin.   II – 69

Fear of the foreigner is what gives rise to hatred. Fear gone, there can be no hatred. Thus his conversion implies our conversion too. If we cease to be inferiors, he cannot be our superior. His arsenals and his weapons, typified in their extreme by the atom bomb, should have no terror for us. It follows that we should not covet them.   II – 74

If non-violence does not appeal to your heart, you should discard it.
II – 134

If the people are not ready for the exercise of the non-violence of the brave, they must be ready for the use of force in self-defense. There should be no camouflage. . . . It must never be secret.   II – 146

To take the name of non-violence when there is a sword in your heart is not only hypocritical and dishonest but cowardly.   II – 153

There is nothing more demoralizing than fake non-violence of the weak and impotent.   II – 153

SECTION THREE

The Spiritual Dimensions of Non-Violence

Gandhi firmly believes that non-violence is actually more natural to man than violence. His doctrine is built on this confidence in man's natural disposition to love. However, man finds himself deeply wounded, and his inmost dispositions are no longer fully true to themselves. In man's disordered condition, violence seems to be the very foundation of social order and is "enthroned as if it were an eternal law," so that man is called upon by society to reject love and enter into a mysterious "higher duty," presented as sacrificial and inscrutable, and demanded by the law of force. Hence the extraordinary difficulty of non-violence, which requires a supernatural courage only obtainable by prayer and spiritual discipline. This courage demands nothing short of the ability to face death with complete fearlessness and to suffer without retaliation. Such a program is meaningless and impossible, Gandhi thinks, without belief in God.

In any case, violence is actually the expression of weakness and confusion. A weak man, inclined to violence, acts justly only by accident. It is the non-violent man (and, by extension, the non-violent society) which is consistently fair and just. Therefore a truly free and just society must be constructed on a foundation of non-violence.

Non-resistance is restraint voluntarily undertaken for the good of society. *It is, therefore, an intensely active, purifying, inward force. . . .* It presupposes ability to offer physical resistance.   I – 63

Non-violence is the greatest and most active force in the world. One cannot be passively non-violent. . . . One person who can express *ahimsa* in life exercises a force superior to all the forces of brutality.   I – 113

Non-violence cannot be preached. It has to be practiced.   I – 129

[*Human society is naturally non-violent.*] All society is held together by non-violence, even as the earth is held in her position by gravitation. But when the law of gravitation was discovered the discovery yielded results of which our ancestors had no knowledge. Even so when society is deliberately constructed in accordance with the law of non-violence, its structure will be different in material particulars from what it is today. . . . What is happening today is disregard of the law of non-violence and enthronement of violence as if it were an eternal law.   I – 198

I know that the progress of non-violence is seemingly a terribly slow progress. But experience has taught me it is the surest way to the common goal.   I – 211

My faith in the saying that what is gained by the sword will also be lost by the sword is imperishable.   I – 212

Non-violence is impossible without self-purification.   I – 245

My greatest weapon is mute prayer.   I – 251

In the composition of the truly brave there should be no malice, no anger, no distrust, no fear of death or physical hurt. Non-violence is certainly not for those who lack these essential qualities.   I – 253

Mental violence has no potency and injures only the person whose thoughts are violent. It is otherwise with mental non-violence. It has potency which the world does not yet know. And what I want is non-violence of thought and deed.   I – 256

Self-respect and honor cannot be protected by others. They are for each individual himself or herself to guard.   I – 260

If we remain non-violent, hatred will die as everything does, from disuse.   I – 263

It is the law of love that rules mankind. Had violence, i.e., hate ruled us, we should have become extinct long ago. And yet the tragedy of it is that the so-called civilized men and nations conduct themselves as if the basis of society was violence.   I – 266

Democracy can only be saved through non-violence, because democracy, so long as it is sustained by violence, cannot provide for or protect the weak. My notion of democracy is that under it the weakest should have the same opportunity as the strongest. This can never happen except through non-violence. . . . Western democracy, as it functions today, is diluted nazism or fascism.   I – 269

Non-violent defense presupposes recklessness about one's life and property.   I – 271

The immovable force of *satyagraha*—suffering without retaliation. I – 272

Those who die unresistingly are likely to still the fury of violence by their wholly innocent sacrifice.   I – 278

He who meets death without striking a blow fulfills his duty cent per cent. The result is in God's hands.   I – 284

If intellect plays a large part in the field of violence, I hold that it plays a larger part in the field of non-violence.   I – 291

As non-violence admits of no grossness, no fraud, no malice, it must raise the moral tone of the defenders. Hence there will be a corresponding rise in the moral tone of the "weak majority" to be defended.   I – 307

Moral support cannot really be given in the sense of giving. It automatically comes to him who is qualified to take it. And such a one can take it in abundance.   I – 315

A *satyagrahi* is dead to his body even before his enemy attempts to kill him, i.e., he is free from attachment to his body and only lives in the victory of his soul. Therefore when he is already thus dead, why should

he yearn to kill anyone? To die in the act of killing is in essence to
die defeated.   I – 318

The general of a non-violent army has got to have greater presence of
mind than that of a violent army, and God would bless him with the
necessary resourcefulness to meet new situations as they arise.   I – 325

A non-violent army need not have the resourcefulness or understanding
of its general, but they will have a perfect sense of discipline to carry
out faithfully his orders.   I – 326

In this age of democracy it is essential that desired results are achieved
by the collective effort of the people. It will no doubt be good to
achieve an objective through the effort of an supremely powerful individual, but it can never make the community conscious of its corporate
strength.   I – 342

If freedom has got to come, it must be obtained by our own internal
strength, by our closing our ranks, by unity between all sections of the
community.   I – 351

A weak man is just by accident. A strong but non-violent man is unjust
by accident.   I – 354

If liberty and democracy are to be truly saved, they will only be by non-
violent resistance no less brave, no less glorious, than violent resistance.
And it will be infinitely braver and more glorious because it will give
life without taking any.   I – 357

When in the face of an upheaval such as we are witnessing there are only a few individuals of immovable faith, they have to live up to their faith even though they may produce no visible effect on the course of events. They should believe that their action will produce tangible results in due course.   I – 381

Such non-violent resisters will calmly die wherever they are but will not bend the knee before the aggressor. They will not be deceived by promises. They do not seek deliverance from the British yoke through the help of a third party [the Japanese]. They believe implicitly in their own way of fighting and no other. Their fight is on behalf of the dumb millions who do not perhaps know that there is such a thing as deliverance. They have neither hatred for the British nor love for the Japanese. They wish well to both as to all others. They would like both to do what is right. They believe that non-violence alone will lead men to do right under all circumstances.   I – 398

The task before the votaries of non-violence is very difficult, but no difficulty can baffle men who have faith in their mission.   I – 398

The best preparation for and even the expression of non-violence lies in the determined pursuit of the constructive program. . . . He who has no belief in the constructive program has, in my opinion, no concrete feeling for the starved millions. He who is devoid of that feeling cannot fight non-violently. In actual practice the expansion of my non-violence has kept exact pace with that of my identification with starved humanity.
                                                         I – 399

Non-violence knows no defeat. It must, however, be true non-violence, not a make-believe.   II – 8

A *satyagrahi* must always be ready to die with a smile on his face, without retaliation and without rancor in his heart. Some people have come to have a wrong notion that *satyagraha* means only jail-going, perhaps facing blows, and nothing more. Such *satyagraha* cannot bring independence. To win independence you have to learn the art of dying without killing. II – 21

Must I do all the evil I can before I learn to shun it? Is it not enough to know the evil to shun it? If not, we should be sincere enough to admit that we love evil too well to give it up. II – 74

A *satyagrahi* cannot wait or delay action till perfect conditions are forthcoming. He will act with whatever material is at hand, purge it of dross and convert it into pure gold. II – 110

Truth and non-violence are not possible without a living belief in God, meaning a self-existent, all-knowing, living Force which inheres in every other force known to the world and which depends on none, and which will live when all other forces may conceivably perish or cease to act. I am unable to account for my life without belief in this all-embracing living Light. II – 112

Crime is a disease like any other malady and is a product of the prevalent social system. Therefore [in a non-violent India] all crime including murder will be treated as a disease. II – 123

Murder can never be avenged by either murder or taking compensation. The only way to avenge murder is to offer oneself as a willing sacrifice, with no desire for retaliation. II – 131

In this age of the atom bomb unadulterated non-violence is the only force that can confound all the tricks of violence put together.   II – 143

The lawlessness, if it can be so described, that I have advocated is like prescribing wholesome and necessary food for the body. Behind my "lawlessness" there is discipline, construction and well-being of society. It is an effective protest against an unjust and injurious law or act. It can never take the form of selfish evasion of duty.   II – 152

SECTION FOUR

The Political Scope of Non-Violence

Gandhi does not envisage a tactical non-violence confined to one area of life or to an isolated moment. His non-violence is a creed which embraces all of life in a consistent and logical network of obligations. One cannot be violent, for example, in interpersonal or family relations, and non-violent with regard to conscription and war. Genuine non-violence means not only non-cooperation with glaring social evils, but also the renunciation of benefits and privileges that are implicitly guaranteed by forces which conscience cannot accept.

Austere political implications of the non-violent way of life are suggested in some of these texts.

So long as I lived under a system of government based on force and voluntarily partook of the many facilities and privileges it created for me, I was bound to help that government to the extent of my ability when it was engaged in a war, *unless I non-cooperated with that government and renounced to the utmost of my capacity the privileges it offered me.*   I – 73

There is no escape for any of us save through truth and non-violence. I know that war is wrong, is an unmitigated evil. I know too that it has got to go. I firmly believe that freedom won through bloodshed or fraud is no freedom.   I – 75

Merely to refuse military service is not enough. . . . This is [to act] after all the time for combating evil is practically gone.   I – 106

Non-cooperation in military service and service in non-military matters are not compatible.   I – 108

Non-violence to be a creed has to be all-pervasive. I cannot be non-violent about one activity of mine and violent about others. That would be a policy, not a life force. [1935]   I – 110

[*Non-Violence in Great Nations?*]
If they can shed the fear of destruction, if they disarm themselves, they will automatically help the rest to regain their sanity. But then these great powers will have to give up their imperialistic ambitions and their exploitation of the so-called uncivilized or semi-civilized nations of the earth and revise their mode of life. It means a complete revolution.
                                                                                 I – 158

The states that are today nominally democratic have either to become frankly totalitarian or, if they are to be truly democratic, they must become courageously non-violent.   I – 159

Peace will never come until the great powers courageously decide to disarm themselves.   I – 176

Don't listen to friends when the Friend inside you says "Do this!"
                                    I – 182

Without the recognition of non-violence on a national scale there is no such thing as a constitutional or democratic government.   I – 199

Democratic government is a distant dream so long as non-violence is not recognized as a living force, an inviolable creed, not a mere policy.
                                    I – 200

[*True Democracy*]
The true democrat is he who with purely non-violent means defends his liberty and therefore his country's and ultimately that of the whole of mankind. In the coming test pacifists have to prove their faith by resolutely refusing to do anything with war, whether of defense or offense. But the duty of resistance accrues only to those who believe in non-violence as a creed—not to those who will calculate and will examine the merits of each case and decide whether to approve or oppose a particular war. It follows that such resistance is a matter for each person to decide for himself and under the guidance of an inner voice, if he recognizes its existence.   I – 204

You cannot build non-violence on a factory civilization. . . . Rural economy as I have conceived it eschews exploitation altogether, and exploitation is the essence of violence. You have therefore to be rural-minded before you can be non-violent, and to be rural-minded you have to have faith in the spinning wheel. I – 243

Morality is contraband in war. I – 268

The cause of liberty becomes a mockery if the price to be paid is the wholesale destruction of those who are to enjoy liberty. I – 272

[*Fields of non-violence*]
1) Resistance to constituted authority.
2) *Ahimsa* in civil (internal) disturbances.
3) External invasion. I – 284

Nobody can practice perfect non-violence. . . . We may not be perfect in our use of it, but we definitely discard the use of violence and grow from failure to success. I – 292

Not all legislation is violence. Legislation imposed by people upon themselves is non-violence to the extent that it is possible in society. . . . That state is perfect and non-violent where the people are governed the least. The European democracies are to my mind the negation of democracy. I – 292

Not to yield your mind means that you will not give way to any temptation. . . . A weak-minded man can never be a *satyagrahi*. The latter's "no" is invariably a "no" and his "yes" an eternal "yes." Such a man alone has the strength to be a devotee of truth and *ahimsa*. But here one must know the difference between steadfastness and obstinacy. If after having said "yes" or "no" one finds out that the decision was wrong and in spite of that knowledge clings to it, that is obstinacy and folly.   I–317

The meaning of refusal to own allegiance is clear. You will not bow to the supremacy of the victor. You will not help him to attain his object.   I–317

The ideally non-violent state will be an ordered anarchy.   I–324

If this conflagration [World War II] is to be put out through non-violent effort, it will be done only by India.   I–342

The leaders of course know what they are fighting for [World War II]. I make no admission that they are right. But neither the English nor the Germans nor the Italians know what they are fighting for except that they trust their leaders and therefore follow them. I submit that this is not enough when the stake is so bloody and staggering as during the present war. . . . When I asked the British soldiers in South Africa during the Boer War they could not tell me what they were fighting for.   I–356

What difference does it make to the dead, the orphans and the home-less, whether the mad destruction is wrought under the name of totali-tarianism or the holy name of liberty or democracy?   I–357

Liberty and democracy become unholy when their hands are dyed red with innocent blood.   I–357

Non-cooperation with evil is a sacred duty.   I – 358

A soldier of peace, unlike the one of the sword, has to give all his spare time to the promotion of peace alike in war time as in peace time. His work in peace time is both a measure of prevention of, as also that of preparation for, war time.   I – 366

I see coming the day of the rule of the poor, whether that rule be through force of arms or of non-violence.   I – 373

You cannot successfully fight them [the Big Powers] with their own weapons. After all, you cannot go beyond the atom bomb. Unless we have a new way of fighting imperialism of all brands in place of the outworn one of violent rising, there is no hope for the oppressed races of the earth.   II – 8

[*To Africans*] The moment the slave resolves that he will no longer be a slave, his fetters fall. He frees himself and shows the way to others. Freedom and slavery are mental states. Therefore the first thing is to say to yourself, "I shall no longer accept the role of a slave. I shall not obey orders as such but shall disobey when they are in conflict with my conscience." The so-called master may lash you and try to force you to serve him. You will say, "No, I will not serve you for your money or under a threat." This may mean suffering. Your readiness to suffer will light the torch of freedom which can never be put out.   II – 10

One day the black races will rise like the avenging Attila against their white oppressors unless someone presents to them the weapon of *satya-graha*.   II – 12

The real "white man's burden" is not insolently to dominate colored or black people under the guise of protection, it is to desist from the hypocrisy which is eating into them. It is time white men learned to treat every human being as their equal.   II – 16

The West is passing through a purgatory today [1946]. Those who have won the war have found that they are no more victors than those who have lost it. Yet it is not in World War II that Western civilization will have met its grave. It is being dug in South Africa. The white civilization in South Africa looks black in contrast with the colored or Asiatic civilization which is comparatively white. If our people remain steadfast and non-violent till the end, I have not a shadow of a doubt that their heroic struggle will drive the last nail in the coffin of Western civilization, which is being found out in its true colors in South Africa.
                                                                                                II – 24

Jesus was an Asiatic. If He was reborn and went to South Africa today and lived there, He would have to live in a ghetto.   II – 25

Those who agree that racial inequality must be removed and yet do nothing to fight the evil are impotent. I cannot have anything to say to such people. After all, the underdogs will have to earn their own salvation.   II – 28

No government on earth can make men who have realized freedom in their hearts salute against their will.   II – 38

A reformer has to sail not with the current. Very often he has to go against it even though it may cost him his life.   II – 39

The real love is to love them that hate you, to love your neighbor even though you distrust him. I have sound reasons for distrusting the English official world. If my love is sincere, I must love the Englishman in spite of my distrust. Of what avail is my love if it be only so long as I trust my friend? Even thieves do that. They become enemies immediately their trust is gone.   II – 42

As the author of fasting as a weapon in *satyagraha* I must state that I cannot give up an opinion honestly held even if the whole world fasts against me. I might as well give up my belief in God because a body of atheists fasted against such belief.   II – 46

I do not appreciate any underground activity. Millions cannot go underground. Millions need not.   II – 50

Mankind is at the crossroads. It has to make its choice between the law of the jungle and the law of humanity.   II – 56

Ahimsa calls for the strength and courage to suffer without retaliation, to receive blows without returning any. But that does not exhaust its meaning. Silence becomes cowardice when occasion demands speaking out the whole truth and acting accordingly.   II – 57

You are no *satyagrahis* if you remain silent or passive spectators while your enemy is being done to death. You must protect him even at the cost of your own life.   II – 63

To benefit by others' killing and delude oneself into the belief that one is being very religious and non-violent is sheer self-deception.   II – 68

I shall bring about economic equality through non-violence by converting the people to my point of view by harnessing the forces of love as against hatred. . . . For that I have to reduce myself to the level of the poorest of the poor.   II – 73

We have all—rulers and ruled—been living so long in a stifling, unnatural atmosphere that we might well feel in the beginning that we have lost the lungs for breathing the invigorating ozone of freedom.

II – 75

A strike should be spontaneous and not manipulated. If it is organized without any compulsion there would be no chance for *goondaism* [hooliganism] and looting. Such a strike would be characterized by perfect cooperation among the strikers. It should be peaceful and there should be no show of force. The strikers should take up some work either singly or in cooperation with each other in order to earn their bread.   II – 80

There should be no strike which is not justifiable on merits. No unjust strike should succeed. All public sympathy must be withheld from such strikes.   II – 81

Strikes for economic betterment should never have a political end as an ulterior motive.   II – 81

Political strikes must be treated on their own merits and must never be mixed with or related to economic strikes.   II – 82

Under no circumstances can India and England give non-violent resistance a reasonable chance while they are both maintaining full military efficiency.   II – 92

If India became the slave of the machine, then, I say, heaven save the world.   II – 99

In this structure [of the new non-violent India] composed of innumerable villages, there will be ever widening, never ascending circles. Life will not be a pyramid with the apex sustained by the bottom. But it will be an oceanic circle whose center will be the individual always ready to perish for the village, the latter ready to perish for the circle of villages, till at last the whole becomes one life composed of individuals, never aggressive in their arrogance but ever humble, sharing the majesty of the oceanic circle of which they are integral units.   II – 112

[*"Their Socialism"*] Their one aim is material progress. Under their socialism there is no individual freedom. You own nothing, not even your body. You may be arrested at any time, though you may have committed no crime. They may send you wherever they like.

[*"My Socialism"*] I was a socialist before many of them were born. My claim will live when their socialism is dead. My socialism means "even unto this last." I do not want to rise on the ashes of the blind, the deaf and the dumb. . . . I want freedom for full expression of my personality. I must be free to build a staircase to Sirius if I want to. . . . My socialism means that the state does not own everything.   II – 116-17

High thinking is inconsistent with complicated material life based on high speed imposed on us by Mammon worship.   II – 121

Without having to enumerate key industries, I would have state ownership where a large number of people have to work together. The ownership of the products of their labor, whether skilled or unskilled, will vest in them through the state.   II – 121

We are all thieves, but most of us are tolerant towards ourselves and intolerant towards those that are found out and are not of the ordinary run. What is a man if he is not a thief who openly charges as much as he can for the goods he sells?   II – 124

A *satyagrahi* will not report a criminal [who has injured him] to the police. He will not try to ride two horses at a time, viz., to pretend to follow the law of *satyagraha* while at the same time seeking police aid. He must forswear the latter in order to follow the former. . . . A reformer cannot afford to be an informer.   II – 126

It is difficult but not impossible to conduct strictly honest business. What is true is that honesty is incompatible with the amassing of a large fortune.   II – 127

The democracies regard army men as their saviors. They bring wealth and subjugate other countries and sustain authority in times of civil disturbance. What is therefore to be wished is that democracy, to be true, should cease to rely on the army for anything whatsoever.   II – 139

War is a respectable term for *goondaism* [hooliganism] practiced on a mass or national scale.   II – 149

You are very much mistaken if you imagine that true democracy obtains either in America or England. The voice of the people may be said to be God's voice . . . But how can there be the voice of God where the people themselves are the exploiters as England and America are? They live on the colored races by exploiting them.   II – 151

I have friends among the Communists. Some of them are like sons to me. But it seems they do not make any distinction between fair and foul, truth and falsehood. . . . They seem to take their instructions from Russia, which they regard as their spiritual home rather than India. I cannot countenance this dependence on an outside power.   II – 155

Intellectual work is important and has an undoubted place in the scheme of life. But what I insist on is the necessity of physical labor. No man, I claim, ought to be free from that obligation.   II – 216

The essence of true religious teaching is that one should serve and befriend all. It is easy enough to be friendly to one's friends. But to befriend the one who regards himself as your enemy is the quintessence of true religion. The other is mere business.   II – 248

Rights that do not flow from duty well performed are not worth having.   II – 269

Impure means result in an impure end.   II – 274

Harbor impurity of mind or body and you have untruth and violence in you.   II – 274

Only truthful, non-violent and pure-hearted socialists will be able to establish a socialistic society in India and the world. To my knowledge there is no country in the world which is purely socialistic.   II – 274

Truth and *ahimsa* must incarnate in socialism. In order that they can, the votary must have a living faith in God. Mere mechanical adherence to truth and *ahimsa* is likely to break down at the critical moment. . . . God is a living Force. . . . He who denies the existence of that great Force denies to himself the use of that inexhaustible Power and thus remains impotent. . . . The socialism of such takes them nowhere.

II – 275

SECTION FIVE

The Purity of Non-Violence

Non-violence must not be vitiated by the desire of human recognition or personal advantage. On the other hand it must lend itself to every form of service and sacrifice that really contributes to the preservation and betterment of human life. It is deeply concerned with the dignity, the freedom, and the well-being of man, especially of the underprivileged. Non-violence is not merely a selfish and negative evasion of responsibility. It is the highest kind of sacrifice for unity and peace.

Gandhi touches on the training of the non-violent resister, and stresses that the use of certain means such as fasting must be marked by prudence and flexibility.

The Mahatma finally faces the failure of his non-violent campaign in India, but declares that the failure was partly his own, partly the fault of his followers. Their motives and conduct were not sufficiently pure. It was, then, not *satyagraha* that had failed but those who used it as a policy for pragmatic ends instead of living by it as a spiritual creed.

Gandhi retained to the end his hope that only genuine non-violence could guarantee the peace and order of the world. But he admitted the uselessness of a purely negative and passive resistance lacking the dynamic, positive, and, above all, spiritual qualities of true *ahimsa*.

[*Non-violent opposition*]
1) It implies not wishing ill.
2) It includes total refusal to cooperate with or participate in activities of the unjust group, even to eating food that comes from them.
3) It is of no avail to those without living faith in the God of love and love for all mankind.
4) He who practices it must be ready to sacrifice everything except his honor.
5) It must pervade *everything* and not be applied merely to isolated acts.   I – 119

[*Politics and Religion*]
I could not be leading a religious life unless I identified myself with the whole of mankind, and that I could not do unless I took part in politics. The whole gamut of man's activities today constitutes an indivisible whole. You cannot divide social, economic, political and purely religious work into watertight compartments.   I – 170

Our experience was that those who went to jail in a prayerful spirit came out victorious, those who had gone on their own strength failed. There is no room for self-pitying in it either, when you say God is giving you the strength. Self-pity comes when you do a thing for which you expect recognition from others. But here there is no question of recognition.
I – 187

While you will keep yourself aloof from all violence, you will not shirk danger. You will rush forth if there is an outbreak of an epidemic or a fire to be combated and distinguish yourself by your surpassing courage and non-violent heroism.   I – 189

There can be degrees in violence, not in non-violence. The constant effort of the votary of non-violence is to purge himself of hatred toward the so-called enemy. There is no such thing as shooting out of love.   I – 190

Non-violence succeeds only when we have a living faith in God.   I – 191

Ahimsa is the most efficacious in front of the greatest *himsa*. Its quality is really tested only in such cases. Sufferers need not see the result. . . .
                                                                    I – 205

In the dictionary of *satyagraha* there is no enemy.   I – 216

Human dignity is best preserved not by developing the capacity to deal destruction but by refusing to retaliate. If it is possible to train millions in the black art of violence, which is the law of the beast, it is more possible to train them in the white art of non-violence, which is the law of regenerate man.   I – 228

It is permissible for, it is even the duty of, a believer in *ahimsa* to distinguish between the aggressor and the defender. Having done so, he will side with the defender in a non-violent manner, i.e., give his life in saving him.   I – 238

It is open to a war resister to judge between the combatants and wish success to the one who has justice on his side. By so judging he is more likely to bring peace between the two than by remaining a mere spectator.
                                                                    I – 241

Unless you have nothing but brotherliness for those that despitefully use you, your resolution that you would stand by the principle of non-violence through thick and thin will have no meaning.   I – 243

Non-violence is not a cloistered virtue confined only to the *rishi* [a holy man, sage]. . . . It is capable of being practiced by the millions, not with full knowledge of its implications but because it is the law of our species.   I – 243

The first condition of non-violence is justice all around in every department of life. Perhaps it is too much to expect of human nature. I do not, however, think so. No one should dogmatize about the capacity of human nature for degradation or exaltation.   I – 267

We have to court death without retaliation and with no malice or anger towards those who bring about disorder.   I – 277

This truly non-violent action is not possible unless it springs from a heart belief that he whom you fear and regard as a robber . . . and you are one, and that therefore it is better that you should die at his hands than that he, your ignorant brother, should die at yours.   I – 279

[*Ahimsa*] is impossible without charity—unless one is saturated with charity. It is only he who feels one with his opponent that can receive his blows as though they were so many flowers. Even one such man, if God favors him, can do the work of a thousand. It requires soul-force—moral courage—of the highest type.   I – 284

The best field for the operation of non-violence—the family or institution regarded as a family. Non-violence between the members of such families should be easy to practice. If that fails it means we have not developed the capacity for pure non-violence.   I– 299

The alphabet of *ahimsa* is best learned in the domestic school, and I can say from experience that if we secure success there we are sure to do so everywhere else. For a non-violent person the whole world is one family. He will thus fear none, nor will others fear him.   I – 299

Two basic maxims for non-violence:
1) *Ahimsa* is the supreme Law or *Dharma*.
2) There is no other Law or *Dharma* than Truth.   I – 301

The first step toward non-violence is firmly to resolve that all untruth and violence shall hereafter be taboo to us, whatever sacrifice it might seem to involve.   I – 301

A votary of *ahimsa* will of course base upon non-violence all his relations with his parents, his children, his wife, his servants, his dependents, etc. But the real test will come at the time of political or communal disturbances or under the menace of thieves and dacoits. Mere resolve to lay down one's life under the circumstances is not enough. There must be the necessary qualification for making the sacrifice. If I am a Hindu, I must fraternize with the Moslems and the rest. In my dealings with them I may not make any distinction between my co-religionists and those who might belong to a different faith. I would seek opportunities to serve them without any feeling of fear or unnaturalness. The word "fear" can have no place in the dictionary of *ahimsa*. Having thus qualified himself by his selfless service, a votary of pure *ahimsa* will be in a position to make a fit offering of himself in a communal conflagration. Similarly, to meet the menace of thieves and dacoits he will need to go among, and cultivate friendly relations with, the communities from which thieves and dacoits generally come.   I – 302

Not to yield your soul to the conqueror means that you will refuse to do that which your conscience forbids you to do. Suppose the "enemy" were to ask you to rub your nose on the ground or to pull your ears or to go through such humiliating performances, you will not submit to any of these humiliations. But if he robs you of your possessions, you will yield them because as a votary of *ahimsa* you have from the beginning decided that earthly possessions have nothing to do with your soul.

I – 317

I have known many meat eaters to be far more non-violent than vegetarians. I – 323

For the individual [non-violent person] the golden rule is that he will *own* nothing. If I decided to settle and walk among the so-called criminal tribes, I should go to them without any belongings and depend on them for my food and shelter. The moment they feel that I am in their midst in order to serve them, they will be my friends. In that attitude is true *ahimsa*. I – 328

Just as one must learn the art of killing in the training for violence, so one must learn the art of dying in the training for non-violence. I – 335

Personally I would not kill insects, scorpions or even snakes. Nor would I under any circumstances take meat. But I may not impose the creed of such *ahimsa* on the Congress. The Congress is not a religious institution; it is a political organization. Its non-violence is limited to human beings. . . . Unlimited *ahimsa* will take time to be universalized. We will have ample cause to congratulate ourselves if we learn to substitute the law of love in society for that of the jungle and if, instead of harboring ill-will and enmity in our bosoms against those whom we regard as our enemies, we learn to love them as actual and potential friends. I – 343

Let us be clear regarding the language we use and the thoughts we nurture. For what is language but the expression of thought? Let your thought be accurate and truthful, and you will hasten the advent of *swaraj* [self-rule] even if the whole world is against you.   I – 353

[*Non-violent resistance in case of a Japanese invasion*] Non-violent resisters would refuse them any help, even water. For it is no part of their duty to help anyone steal their country. . . . Suppose the Japanese compel the resisters to give them water, the resisters must die in the act of resistance. . . . The underlying belief in such non-violent resistance is that the aggressor will, in time, be mentally and physically tired of killing non-violent resisters. He will begin to search what this new (for him) force is which refuses cooperation without seeking to hurt, and will probably desist from further slaughter. But the resister may find that the Japanese are utterly heartless and that they do not care how many they kill. The non-violent resisters will have won the day inasmuch as they will have preferred extermination to submission.   I – 397

There is a natural prejudice against fasting as part of a political struggle. . . . It is considered a vulgar interpolation in politics by the ordinary politician, though it has always been resorted to by prisoners. . . . My own fasts have always been strictly according to the laws of *satyagraha*. . . . I have been driven to the conclusion that fasting unto death is an integral part of the *satyagraha* program, and it is the greatest and most effective weapon in its armory under given circumstances. Not everyone is qualified for undertaking it without a proper course of training.
                                                                    I – 411, 412

A *satyagrahi* should fast only as a last resort when all other avenues of redress have been explored and have failed.   II – 48

There is no room for imitation in fasts. He who has no inner strength should not dream of it, and never with attachment to success. But if a *satyagrahi* once undertakes a fast from conviction, he must stick to his resolve whether there is a chance of his action bearing fruit or not. . . .

He who fasts in the expectation of fruit generally fails. And even if he does not seemingly fail, he loses all the inner joy which a true fast holds. II – 48

It is wrong to fast for selfish ends, e.g., for an increase in one's own salary. Under certain circumstances it is permissible to fast for an increase in wages on behalf of one's group. II – 49

Ridiculous fasts spread like plague and are harmful. II – 49

Shopkeepers, traders, mill-hands, laborers, farmers, clerks, in short, everyone, ought to consider it his or her duty to get the necessary training in *satyagraha*. II – 60

I am not able to accept in its entirety the doctrine of non-killing of animals. I have no feeling in me to save the life of these animals who devour or cause hurt to man. I consider it wrong to help in the increase of their progeny. . . . To do away with monkeys where they have become a menace to the well-being of man is pardonable. II – 67

Prayer is not an old woman's idle amusement. Properly understood and applied, it is the most potent instrument of action. II – 77

Non-Violent Volunteer Corps
　　They must be small if they are to be efficient.
　　The members must know one another well.
　　Each corps will select its own head.
One thing should be common to all members and that is implicit faith in God. He is the only companion and doer. Without faith in Him these peace brigades will be lifeless.

[*Rules for peace brigades*]
  1) A volunteer may not carry any weapons.
  2) The members of a corps must be easily recognizable.
  3) Every volunteer must carry bandages, scissors, needle and thread, surgical knife, etc., for rendering first aid.
  4) He should know how to carry and remove the wounded.
  5) He should know how to put out fires, how to enter a fire area without getting burnt, how to climb heights for rescue work and descend safely with or without his charge.
  6) He should be well acquainted with all the residents of his locality. This is a service in itself.
  7) He should pray [with the Name of God] ceaselessly in his heart and persuade others who believe to do likewise.   II – 86, 87

The positively necessary training for a non-violent army is an immovable faith in God, willing and perfect obedience to the chief of the non-violent army, and perfect inward and outward cooperation between the units of the army.   II – 92

An unjust law is itself a species of violence. Arrest for its breach is more so. Now the law of non-violence says that violence should be resisted not by counter-violence but by non-violence. . . . This I do by breaking the law and by peacefully submitting to arrest and imprisonment.   II – 150

Fasting cannot be undertaken mechanically. It is a powerful thing but a dangerous thing if handled amateurishly. It requires complete self-purification, much more than is required in facing death with retaliation even in mind.   II – 165

The minimum that is required of a person wishing to cultivate the *ahimsa* of the brave is first to clear one's thought of cowardice and in the light of this clearance regulate his conduct in every activity, great or small. Thus the votary must refuse to be cowed down by his superior, without being angry. He must, however, be ready to sacrifice his post however remunerative it may be. While sacrificing his all, if the votary has no sense of irritation against his employer, he has *ahimsa* of the brave in him.   II – 176

Things that have been done under pressure of a fast have been undone after the fast is over. What a spiritual fast does expect is cleansing of the heart.   II – 362

In the secret of my heart I am in perpetual quarrel with God that He should allow such things [as the war] to go on. My non-violence seems almost impotent. But the answer comes at the end of the daily quarrel that neither God nor non-violence is impotent. Impotence is in men. I must try on without losing faith even though I may break in the attempt.   I – 213

Indian non-violence has brought no relief to the cultured Western powers because it is still poor stuff. Why travel so far to see its inefficacy? . . . Not until the Congress or a similar group of people represents the non-violence of the strong will the world catch the infection.   I – 267

If I am a true teacher of *ahimsa*, I am sure you will soon leave behind your teacher. If that does not happen, it will only mean that I was an unfit teacher. But if my teaching fructifies, there will be teachers of *ahimsa* in every home.   I – 290

In placing civil disobedience before constructive work I was wrong, and I did not profit by the Himalayan blunder that I had committed.
                                                        I – 291

My imperfections and failures are as much a blessing from God as my successes and my talents, and I lay them both at His feet.   I – 291

Today [1940] we are not even within ken of the *ahimsa* of the strong [i.e., not ready for civil disobedience].   I – 300

The Congress has not had a living faith in non-violence. Therefore the non-violence of the Congress has really been non-violence of the weak.   I – 371

Several lives like mine will have to be given if the terrible violence that has spread all over is to stop and non-violence reign supreme in its place.   II – 133

So long as we have not cultivated the strength to die with courage and love in our hearts, we cannot hope to develop the *ahimsa* of the strong.   II – 136

The mind of a man who remains good under compulsion cannot improve, in fact it worsens.   II – 138

The more I practice it the clearer I see how far I am from the full expression of *ahimsa* in my life.   II – 143

Non-violence is today [Hindu-Moslem hostility] rightly laughed out of court as Utopian. Nevertheless, I maintain that it is the only way to keep Hinduism alive and India undivided.   II – 154

Our non-violence is as yet a mixed affair. It limps. Nevertheless, it is there and it continues to work like a leaven in a silent and invisible way, least understood by most. It is the only way.   II – 166

[With respect to unrest and riots in India, 1942–1946, had non-violence failed?] That [violence] can never mean that the creed of non-violence has failed. At best it may be said that I have not yet found the technique required for the conversion of the mass mind.   II – 176

I have no wish to live if India is to be submerged in a deluge of violence as it is threatening to do. . . . I am in the midst of flames. Is it the kindness of God or His irony that the flames do not consume me? (May, 1947)   II – 257

The future will depend on what we do in the present.   II – 259

[At the end of his life Gandhi admitted loss of hope of attaining real non-violence in India.] The loss of hope arises from my knowledge that I have not attained sufficient detachment and control over my temper and emotions which entitle one to entertain the hope. . . . [but] I do not want to harbor the thought of hopelessness.   II – 264

[*Apparent failure of non-violence in India*] I must confess my bankruptcy, not that of non-violence. . . . India has no experience of the non-violence of the strong.   II – 265

My faith is as strong as ever. It is quite possible that my technique is faulty. . . . I can say to all my counselors that they should have patience with me and even share my belief that there is no hope for the aching world except through the narrow and straight path of non-violence. Millions like me may fail to prove the truth in their own lives; that would be their failure, never of the eternal law.   II – 266

I have admitted my mistake. I thought our struggle was based on non-violence, whereas in reality it was no more than passive resistance, which essentially is a weapon of the weak. It leads naturally to armed resistance whenever possible.   II – 276

Non-violence is my creed. It never was of the Congress. With the Congress it has always been a policy.   II – 280

Ahimsa is always infallible. When, therefore, it appears to have failed, the failure is due to the inaptitude of the votary.   II – 294

It is perhaps wrong to describe my present state of mind as depression. . . . I am not vain enough to think that the divine purpose can only be fulfilled through me. It is as likely as not that a fitter instrument will be used to carry it out and that I was good enough to represent a weak nation, not a strong one. May it not be that a man purer, more courageous, more far-seeing is wanted for the final purpose? This is all speculation. No one has the capacity to judge God. We are drops in that limitless ocean of mercy.   II – 321

Mine must be a state of complete resignation to the Divine Will.
                   II – 321

We are daily paying the heavy price for the unconscious mistake we made in mistaking passive resistance for non-violent resistance.   II – 325

I failed to recognize, until it was too late, that what I had mistaken for *ahimsa* was not *ahimsa*, but passive resistance of the weak, which can never be called *ahimsa* even in the remotest sense.   II – 327

[*The fast unto death, January, 1948*] My fast should not be considered a political move in any sense of the term. It is obedience to the peremptory call of conscience and duty. It comes out of felt agony.   II – 363

Notes

1) See the important book, *The Dark Eye in Africa,* with its thesis that the white man's spiritual rejection and contempt for the African is the result of his rejection of what is deepest and most vital in himself. Having "lost his own soul," the materialistic and cunning exploiter of the colonies destroyed the soul of the native. The "one-eyed giant" has "outer vision" only, no "inner vision." Therefore, though he tries to take precautions to avoid spiritual disaster for himself and the races he has subjugated, these precautions are "without perspective" and in "the wrong dimension of reality."

2) L. L. Whyte, *The Next Development in Man* (New York, 1948), p. 122.

3) *Ibid.,* pp. 148, 149, 151.

4) *Ibid.,* p. 169.

5) *Ibid.,* p. 288.

6) *Am I My Brother's Keeper?* (New York, 1947), p. 67.

7) *Ibid.,* p. 64.

8) A. Koyré, *Discovering Plato* (New York, 1945), p. 108.

9) Hannah Arendt, *The Human Condition* (Chicago, 1958), p. 49.

10) *Hindu Dharma* (Ahmedabad, 1958), p. 93.

11) *Ibid.,* p. 35.

12) *Ibid.,* p. 36.

13) "Allocution du P. Monchanin 20 fevrier 1948," in Appendix to C. Drevet, *Pour Connaître la pensée de Gandhi,* 2e edition (Paris, 1954), p. 224.

14) Hannah Arendt, *op. cit.,* p. 121.

15) *Summa Theologica,* II, IIæ, q. 30, art. 1, ad. 1.

16) *Ibid.,* art. 2.

17) *Ibid.,* ad. 3. Cf. St. Thomas Aquinas on the "mood of Nemesis" which "rejoices in the belief that others justly suffer and grieves when good comes to the unworthy," art. 3, ad. 2.

18) Hannah Arendt, *op. cit.,* p. 240.

19) *Ibid.,* p. 241.

20) *Handbook of the Militant Christian,* trans. with an Introduction by John P. Dolan (Notre Dame, 1962).

21) *Shepherd of Hermas* (New York, 1948), pp. 267, 268.

22) "On Being in One's Right Mind," *Review of Religion,* November, 1942.

23) *Shepherd of Hermas,* Fourth Mandate, II. 1, p. 265.

24) *Utrum caecitas mentis sit peccatum, Summa Theologica,* II, IIæ, q. 15, art. 1.

25) *Shepherd of Hermas,* pp. 262-263.

26) Migne, *Patrologia Latina,* 4:604.

27) "Let that by which you were wounded become your own cure." Migne, *op. cit., De Zelo et Livore,* 4:649.

28) *The Gandhi Reader,* ed. by Homer A. Jack (New York, 1961), p. 219.

Index

Erasmus, Desiderius, 15

Evil: Aquinas' analysis of, 12-13; dogma of irreversibility of, 11; non-cooperation with, 9-10, 19, 52, 56; returning good for, 15

Family, as best field for operation of non-violence, 66
Fascism, 5, 45
Fasts, Gandhi's, 8, 16, 58, 69-70, 71, 72, 76
Fear, freedom from, 38, 40, 67
Forgiveness, 17, 18
Freedom, Gandhi's doctrine of, 6, 10, 14-15, 18, 28, 47, 56, 57

God, 26, 29, 31, 32, 34, 38, 39, 46, 47, 49, 61, 64, 65, 66, 73, 74; and *ahimsa,* 25, 43; Gandhi's quarrel with, 72; Gandhi's resignation to Will of, 75; living faith in, required by prayer, 31; and peace brigades, 70, 71; and *satyagraha,* 30; and socialism, 62; as Truth, 27, 28, 33
Goodness, joined with knowledge, 34
Goonda (hooligan, rowdy): 39, 59

Harijan (the untouchables; the outcaste masses): 5, 8, 9, 16
Hijrat (self-imposed exile): 37
Himsa (violence): 23
Hinduism, 8, 9, 73
Hitler, Adolf, 2, 12
Human Condition, The, 7
Humility, and non-violence, 36

India, 6, 9, 10, 14, 16, 19, 49, 55, 59, 60, 61, 72, 73; apparent failure of non-violence in, 74; awakening of spiritual consciousness of, 5; Gandhi's struggle for freedom of, 4, 7, 8; liberated, "vivisection" of, 18, 34; possibilities of non-violence in, 26; riots in (1942-1946), 74; as torch bearer to oppressed, 40
Indifferentism, 4
Injustice, need for resisting, 39
Intellect, in field of non-violence, 46

Japan, 2, 5, 32, 36, 37, 69
John XXIII, 20

Labor, physical, necessity of, 62
Law, natural, 5

BOOKS
by MAHATMA GANDHI

Autobiography

Economic and Industrial Life and Relations (3 volumes)

A Gandhi Anthology (2 volumes)

Hindu Dharma

My Non-Violence

The Problem of Education

Satyagraha

Selected Letters (2 volumes)

The Way to Communal Harmony

Published by the

NAVAJIVAN TRUST

Ahmedabad-14, India

New Directions Paperbooks

Complete descriptive catalog available free on request from
New Directions, 333 Sixth Avenue, New York 10014.

† Bilingual